EDINBURGH

CITY WALKS

Compiled by
Margot McMurdo

Margot McMurdo is a qualified Blue Badge
Scottish Tourist Guide and a highly experienced
and locally-based Edinburgh and Scotland guide.

 # Contents

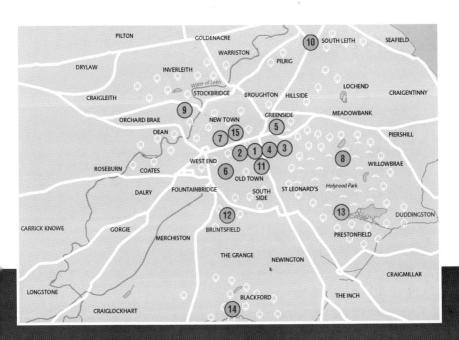

Introduction to City Walks Edinburgh

Edinburgh is a wonderful city, the capital of Scotland and a World Heritage Site. The city is a perfect place to explore on foot, which is the best way to see the variety of architecture from the narrow lanes of the Old Town to the open elegance of the squares and crescents of the Georgian New Town. The city is so steeped in history that with almost every step you take you can discover something of interest and the walks in this guide reveal the most fascinating stories to some of the places, personalities and events that have made the city we see today.

No stay in Edinburgh would be complete without a visit to Edinburgh Castle, pride of the city, perched on top of its volcanic rock. Within its walls are the Scottish Crown Jewels and the Stone of Destiny. Leading down from the Castle is the Royal Mile, actually a little longer than one mile, stretching down through the Old Town to the Palace of Holyroodhouse. The Royal Mile is divided into sections called Castlehill, Lawnmarket, High Street, Canongate and Abbey Strand and with so much to experience, there are four walks along its 1 mile 107 yards.

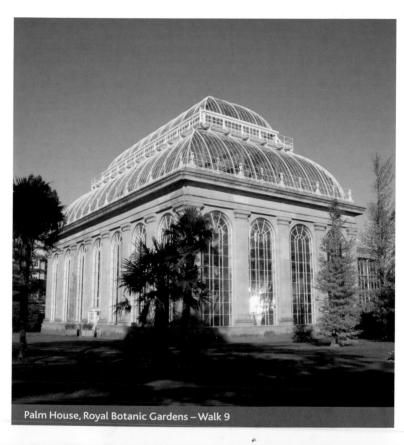

Palm House, Royal Botanic Gardens – Walk 9

Camera Obscura – Walk 1

Land – a Land is the building itself not just the land it is built on.

Pend – an arched passage leading to the back of houses.

Tenement – a tall building of homes with a stair internally to all floors (an early apartment block).

Wynd (pronounced w-eye-nd, not wind) – a narrow street open at both ends.

Leith Walk Giraffes – Walk 10

There may be some words that you will come across that are unfamiliar:-

Cobbles or setts are the blocks of stone on many of the Old and New Town roads. They may be uneven so take care when crossing.

Close – a very narrow lane or vennel leading to the back of some buildings.

Entry – an alleyway between houses.

Bute House – Walk 7

Beyond the city centre of the Old Town, Grassmarket and Greyfriars and the Georgian New Town, the routes take you north to the shores of the Firth of Forth at Leith and to Morningside and Blackford Hill in the south, for wonderful views northward over Edinburgh, and from the Royal Botanic Gardens at Inverleith in the west to Edinburgh's oldest inn at Duddingston village in the east. In between incredible tales are told of the artisans, authors, body-snatchers, golfers, poets, plantsmen, pioneers, medics, monarchs, sportsmen and teachers whose rich legacies have shaped Scotland's capital. Also, do enjoy the pubs, inns and tearooms highlighted en-route and dare to try the infamous Scottish delicacy available at Bene's in Canongate... and it's not haggis!

WITCHES, 'GARDY LOO!' AND DR JEKYLL AND MR HYDE

Royal Mile part 1

WALK 1

This short stroll from one of the city's highest points sets off down the Royal Mile – so named because of the royal residences at each end of the road. Edinburgh Castle is at the top; the Palace of Holyroodhouse at the lower end. It is actually an extra 107 yards longer than a traditional mile of 1,760 yards. There are many historic closes along the Royal Mile and this route explores some of the more intriguing and interesting ones.

Start	Finish	Distance	Refreshments
Castle Esplanade	High Street – Cockburn Street junction	½ mile (800 metres)	Deacon Brodie's Tavern; The Albanach

Glandstone's Land

ON THIS WALK

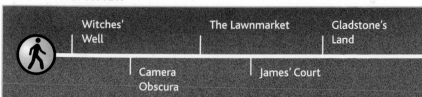

Witches' Well | The Lawnmarket | Gladstone's Land

Camera Obscura | James' Court

Begin on the Castle Esplanade. Originally used as a parade ground for soldiers from the castle, this large open space is home, every August, to the Royal Edinburgh Military Tattoo. The tattoo is a unique display of music and entertainment with Edinburgh Castle as the backdrop. More than 200,000 visitors attend every year. This is not just a Scottish event as performers from 46 countries have entertained over the years. The highlights are the massed bands of bagpipes and drums and the lone piper on the castle battlements.

There are many monuments on the esplanade, but one of the most fascinating is the **Witches' Well.** Walk to the lower left-hand side of the Esplanade with the castle behind you. There is a beautiful bronze drinking fountain on the wall. This commemorates 300 witches who were burned at the stake between 1492 and 1722. The fountain was designed by John Duncan and erected in 1912. Notice a spray of the foxglove plant (digitalis); in the correctly prescribed amount this could aid healing, but was fatal if overdosed. Many centuries ago people were suspicious of those who used plants in medicine, and tended to think of them as witches.

Continue down the left side of the street on the Castlehill section of the Royal Mile. The large building on your left was erected on the site of the old **Reservoir** constructed in 1720, the present building dating from 1849. It held water which was brought five miles from springs at Comiston. The reservoir could hold 2 million gallons of water. It was then piped to other wells located in various places around the Old Town.

On the corner of Ramsay Lane is the **Camera Obscura** or Outlook Tower. The building was originally the town house of Ramsay of Dalhousie, the Laird of Cockpen, which was a 17th century tenement. Maria Theresa Short, an optician, bought it as an observatory that opened to the public in 1853. Sir Patrick Geddes owned the building in 1892 and gave it its present name of the Camera Obscura when he developed it as a sociological museum. From the top of the tower, with the aid of revolving mirrors and lenses, you can see a moving picture of the city below.

Continue down the hill and enter the Lawnmarket section of the Royal Mile. The **Lawnmarket** was a cloth market in 1477. As the 'Landmarket' it sold the produce of the land but on Wednesdays it became a linen and lawn market. Wool was also sold here in the 18th century. It was a very upmarket place to stay in the Old Town and became the residential area for ambassadors to Scotland.

Imagine yourself in the 18th century. The Royal Mile was home to 50,000 people; appalling living conditions prevailed. They did not have the

| Deacon Brodie's Tavern | City Chambers |
| Lady Stair's House | Advocate's Close | Anchor Close |

Leabharlanna Poibli Chathair Bhaile Átha Cliath
WALK 1 – ROYAL MILE PART 1   7
Dublin City Public Libraries

The Witches' Well

but the nickname of the smell of the open sewers of the Old Town.

Keep to the left-hand side of the street to reach an opening to **Milne's Court**. Walk through into the open square. Notice the unusually shaped, almost bell-like railings. This was to enable ladies with fashionable crinoline-style dresses of yesteryear to pass each other safely on the staircase.

Return to the opening and turn left down Lawnmarket. The next entrance on the left is to **James' Court**. In this courtyard notice the 'garages' where sedan chairs were once kept. These were wardrobe-like boxes with windows and a door into a seat. There were two poles attached along the outside so that the sedan chair could be carried by two strong men. They were the 'taxi' of the 18th century for those who could afford a ride.

Continuing down the Lawnmarket there is an interesting building on your left with two archways and an arcade front. This is **Gladstone's Land**. Above the arches is a sign with a golden hawk, a 'gled' – the Scottish name for the bird of prey. It is a play on the name Gledstane as Sir Thomas Gledstane, a wealthy textile merchant, was the owner of the original close in 1631. Gladstone's Land is open to the public. The central part of the building dates from 1550 and the wooden ceiling is from 1620. Sir Thomas lived in only two rooms with his wife, six children and a maid, although he owned the whole building. There are fabrics on display (the Lawnmarket) as the ground floor was used as a shop. Look for a large pig in a comfy box –

sanitary plumbing that is expected as standard today. At 10.00pm every night, a call went around the town of 'gardy loo!' (from the French 'gardez l'eau!' or 'look out for the water!'). This was to warn unfortunate pedestrians that the windows were being flung open and ALL the household waste was about to come cascading down on them. 'Haud yer hand!' ('hold your hand!') would be called back from those in the street below as they ran for cover. Pigs would then rummage about in the debris and the citizens of Edinburgh would pick their way carefully through the stinking rubbish. The stench often crept into the houses so some people burned paper to fumigate their homes. The wealthier people tended to live on the upper floors, as far away from the putrid smells as possible.

In the early morning around 7.00am, scavengers started to clean up the mess except on a Sunday, the day of rest, when the decaying rubbish had to lie until Monday morning. There is a fiddle tune called *The Floors of Edinburgh* (The Flowers of Edinburgh) which is not about a bunch of locally grown flowers

not a real pig but a very convincing model sow.

There were many good reasons for owning a pig in Edinburgh's Old Town: one – it would eventually provide plenty of roast dinners; two – these houses did not have central heating, and there were no duvets or electric blankets, so when it was chilly at night the pig was put into the bed first to warm it up, then removed before bedtime; and three – at night, putting your day clothes over the pig. This was not to keep dear piggy warm but allowed any bugs or fleas to transfer to the animal so you had pest-free clothes to put on in the morning.

One of the rather eccentric court judges, Lord Gardenstone, kept a pet pig. He adored his pig so much he actually slept with it and took it on a lead for walks around the town.

Explore the next opening on the left, Lady Stair's Close. Entering the inner courtyard you will

see **Lady Stair's House**, built in 1622 by wealthy merchant Sir William Gray of Pittendrum. The close was originally named Lady Gray's Close after his wife Geida Smith. Their initials are carved on the lintel above the doorway WG & GS. This is called a marriage lintel. There is also a carved motto 'FEARE THE LORD & DEPART FROM EVIL'.

On another external wall look up to see a carved sign depicting two clasped hands. This is a Fire Mark and was displayed to show that the building was certified in the event of a fire. In the 18th century each insurance company had its own fire brigade, specifically to extinguish fires in the buildings it insured. If you had a house fire and did not display a Fire Mark, the fire could be extinguished but a fee would have to be paid at a later date.

Inside the house, specific steps (quite literally) had been taken to ensure that the owners were safe. The stair itself was the 'burglar alarm'. The worn steps of an Edinburgh tenement are usually

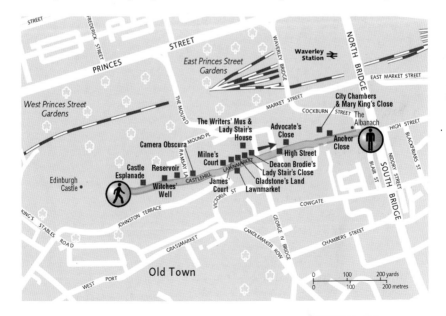

of a uniform height for ease in climbing, but by including a couple of 'trip' steps of a different height a potential burglar might be caught out. As an additional precaution this spiral stair climbs clockwise, so a right-handed swordsman defending his property would have some advantage over a right-handed intruder coming up the stairs.

Eventually the building was left to Elizabeth, Dowager-Countess of Stair, hence its name. Today Lady Stair's House is open to the public and is home to **The Writers' Museum**. The museum displays objects, manuscripts and paintings relating to the lives and works of three great Scottish writers – Robert Burns, Robert Louis Stevenson and Sir Walter Scott.

Just past Wardrop's Court is

one of Edinburgh's most famous pubs, **Deacon Brodie's Tavern**. This hostelry is named after William Brodie (1741-88). During the day he was a pious, wealthy and respected citizen. His trade was cabinet making and he was Deacon of the Incorporation of Wrights and a Town Councillor of the City. Wright is the Scots' name for a cabinet maker. By night he was a thief, gambler and kept two mistresses, both of whom presented him with a family. He needed plenty of money to maintain his lifestyle.

When Brodie delivered an item of furniture he would carry a pad of soft wax in his pocket and make an imprint of the property's key. It was also common for tradespeople to hang their keys on a nail at the back of the shop door, easy pickings for Brodie and his pad of wax. He would have a copy of the keys made in his workshop, then return to the house or shop at a later date to burgle the contents.

Deacon Brodie's Tavern

He plotted to break into the General Excise Office in Chessel's Court. This building contained the money from taxes collected from the King's Scottish subjects. Brodie used his putty to make a copy of the key and he and his gang broke in and ransacked the place, but only managed to steal £16 from the cashier's office. Brodie was a marked man and so he fled the country, but there was a reward of £200 on his head. He was eventually arrested in Amsterdam and brought back to Edinburgh to face trial, which took place on the 27th August 1788.

Brodie was sentenced to death on the 1st October, but he had one last cunning plan. One of his visitors in prison was a doctor who inserted a small metal tube in his throat to prevent suffocation from the hangman's noose. He also had a metal neck-brace made. As an extra precaution, Brodie bribed the hangman to adjust the rope to avoid dislocating his neck. He also had a surgeon on stand-by to revive him after the hanging. But all this was in vain. He was successfully hanged, ironically on the very gibbet made in his workshop. Diagonally across the road junction here is the site of the gallows on that fateful day. It is marked with a brass 'H' on the ground.

A mural painted on the side of the pub tells William Brodie's tale. It is said that the writer Robert Louis Stevenson based his characters of Dr Jekyll and Mr Hyde on the split personality of William Brodie.

Cross Bank Street into the section of the Royal Mile known as the **High Street**. In August there is every possibility that this part of the Royal Mile will be crowded with performers and their audiences as street theatre is part of the Edinburgh Festival and Festival Fringe. There's likely to be musicians, dancers, stilt walkers, jugglers and mime artists.

Carry on down High Street to **Advocate's Close**, believed to date from 1544. It was so narrow that residents could shake hands with their neighbours across the close. An Advocate is the name for a Scottish barrister or attorney. It is one of the most photographed parts of the city as it offers a superb view from the High Street down to Princes Street and the Georgian New Town. The tall dark monument you will see is to Sir Walter Scott.

A little farther down is the **City Chambers**. This building houses various departments of the Edinburgh Council. In the courtyard you will see a huge statue of Emperor Alexander the Great and his horse Bucephalus, which literally means 'bull headed'. The statue represents 'mind over brute force'. It was designed in 1832 and cast in bronze in 1883.

The City Chambers holds one the city's most famous closes, **Mary King's Close**, but it is deep underground and does not appear on any map. Discover more on a pre-booked guided tour, but be warned, it is not for the faint-hearted.

The close is named after Mary, daughter of Alexander King, who lived in the early 17th century. In 1645 there was an outbreak of bubonic plague (Black Death) and it was said it started in this close. Believing this awful disease was carried by the buildings themselves, the whole place was blocked up. It was deserted for 110 years. When again it started to be occupied, there were so many ghostly apparitions that the place was shut once more. Later a fire destroyed part of the area and the City Chambers was built out of the ruins. Now open for the public to view, it's sometimes known as the 'The Street of Sorrows'.

Keep ahead shortly reaching **Anchor Close**, which dates from 1521. It used to contain the Anchor Tavern, the home of a club called the Crochalan Fencibles. The Fencibles were volunteers who were to resist any invasion. One of the members was the poet Robert Burns. The parents of Sir Walter Scott lived here until 1771 and the close also contained a printing house. The Encyclopaedia Britannica was first printed here in 1768.

Walk on to meet the top of Cockburn Street, an interesting street of small shops leading down towards Waverley Station and Princes Street. On the corner here is The Albanach, and as they say on their sign it's, 'a peaceful place in a busy world', so pop in for some post walk refreshment.

Royal Mile part 2

WALK 2

This walk explores the right-hand side of the upper half of the Royal Mile from the Castle, touring Parliament Square and finding the Heart of Midlothian. The route takes in the favourite haunt – still 'visited' – of one of the city's eccentric former inhabitants, and leads to the ghostly presence in Bell's Wynd. You can retrace their steps safely today and find out about other well-known characters that resided here and definitely left their mark on Edinburgh society.

Start	Finish	Distance	Refreshments
Castle Esplanade	High Street – South Bridge junction	½ mile (800 metres)	The Witchery Restaurant; Edinburgh Larder

The Heart of Midlothian

ON THIS WALK

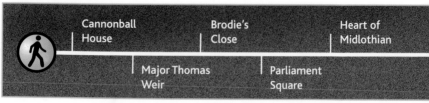

Cannonball House

Major Thomas Weir

Brodie's Close

Parliament Square

Heart of Midlothian

Cannonball House

Start from the foot of the Castle Esplanade, standing on the right-hand side with the castle at your back. Look up at the building that has windows overlooking the Esplanade; this is **Cannonball House**, built in 1630. The house takes its name from a cannonball embedded in the west gable wall. Look carefully to see it above one of the windows. It is said that the cannonball was fired from the castle in 1745 during the Jacobite siege. An alternative explanation is that it marks the gravitation height of Edinburgh's first piped water supply in 1681. Above the door lintel is the religious motto 'O Lord in Thee is al mi Trust' (O Lord in thee is all my trust).

Continue down Castlehill past Cannonball House to **The Scotch Whisky Experience**. This is the story of Scotland's best-known export and the whisky shop was originally the Castlehill School.

Just past the Whisky Centre is **Boswell's Court** named after James Boswell (1740-95) who was born in Edinburgh and became a prominent advocate (lawyer). He was the biographer of Dr Samuel Johnson (1709-84), the lexicographer, and his travels around Scotland with Boswell are well documented. It is said that Boswell lived and dined here with Dr Johnson, but the close is actually named after the main resident and physician, Dr John Boswell, uncle of James Boswell.

The Witchery Restaurant is now the occupant of Boswell's Court, one of the 'hot tickets' for dining in the city. It has accommodation with individually designed atmospheric rooms, such as The Inner Sanctum or Library Bedrooms – reservations are essential. Visitors have commented that as they walk down the close to the Garden Room dining room that they can see where JK Rowling got some of her inspiration for her writings in the Harry Potter books. It can be quite spooky.

The next building on your right is The Highland Tolbooth, St John's Church, completed in 1844 for the General Assembly of the Church of Scotland. It has the highest spire in the city at 240 feet (73 metres). It was taken over in 1984 and is now **The Hub** which

Parliament House | Bell's Wynd

High Kirk of St Giles | Mercat Cross | Tron Kirk

has a cafeteria, shops and exhibition area.

Cross the junction to the shops on the right-hand side of the Lawnmarket. This area was one of the places a notorious Edinburgh character would wander around, **Major Thomas Weir** (1599-1670). He lived with his sister Grizel and he could often be seen out walking, always with his long blackthorn staff. He attended religious meetings and would lead the prayers. At one of the meetings he started to speak about some dreadful foul deeds; deeds he had perpetrated. People said he took orders from his walking stick and that this was bewitched. His sister admitted that her brother had carried out some awful acts. He was eventually hanged and burnt at the stake along with his wicked stick, which it is said danced and jumped in the flames. Major Weir reputedly haunts this area at night.

Continue down Lawnmarket to a statue of Deacon William Brodie, outside the entrance to the Deacon's Coffee House in **Brodie's Close**. This is always a good photo opportunity to link arms with the man who inspired Robert Louis Stevenson to write Dr Jekyll and Mr Hyde. Brodie was a cabinet maker by day and a burglar by night (see Walk1).

Walk into Brodies Close, the café was the original cabinet workshop of William Brodie. There are murals depicting his life and work and it is an excellent place for delicious home baking or a light lunch, to take in the atmosphere of the place and imagine the business that used to be here – 'Brodie & Sons, Wrights & Undertakers'.

At the corner with George IV Bridge is a relatively new building, **The Missoni Hotel**. If you take a quick look around the corner you may see the concierge wearing a very modern kilt design. The zigzag pattern matches the huge ceramic pot in the hotel window; an interesting take on the traditional Scottish Highland dress.

Cross the road called George IV Bridge. Once across, glance down to the ground to find an 'H' shape in brass embedded in the paving. This marks the spot where the gallows once stood and where Deacon Brodie was hanged in 1788.

Just past this brass plate is the large stone block which was once a well. If you could not carry the heavy bucket to your house you could hire the services of a water carrier, a cadie, to do this for you. This term is still in use on the golf course today.

Next on the right is **Parliament Square**.

The square surrounds St Giles' Cathedral – 'the High Kirk of Edinburgh'. In front of the west entrance is the towering memorial to the 5th Duke of Buccleuch (1806-84), Walter Francis Montague Douglas Scott, also known as the 7th Duke of Queensberry. He is depicted in the robes of the Order of the Garter. The figure was carved by Edgar Boehm in 1887-1888 and is more than 10 feet high. It is carved in stone from the Binny Quarry, as it was thought it would weather better than granite and would blend well with the bronze panels. On the hexagonal base are six bucks rampant holding the coats of arms of families related to the Buccleuchs through marriage. The six panels show major events from the Buccleuch family history. There are also six symbolic figures of the virtues of the Duke – Fortitude, Liberality, Temperance, Prudence, Charity and Truth.

The cobbled area behind the Buccleuch Statue is where the horse-drawn Hansom Cabs would park to let down and pick up their passengers from the adjoining courthouse and related buildings. If you look carefully you may find the two brass plates marking the parking stances.

A few steps past the Buccleuch Statue there is a heart-shaped design in the cobbles, **The Heart of Midlothian**. This marks the spot where the Old Tolbooth stood. The building was demolished in 1817 but it stood for over 400 years in several guises, as a council office, a toll-

collection point, a jail and a place of execution. If you look carefully around the area of the heart you will see brass plates that mark the outline of the ancient building. It was a custom for prisoners who had been set free to spit as they passed through the doorway to freedom, and still today it is a peculiar Edinburgh custom to spit on the Heart of Midlothian for luck.

The High Kirk of St Giles stands over Parliament Square. Kirk is a Scottish word for church. The medieval vault and the crown tower date from the 1500s, but were restored in the 17th century. It is worth taking some time to explore inside to see the Thistle Chapel, wonderful stained glass and interesting tombs. There is also a huge statue of **John Knox** (1513-72), the main figure in the Scottish church reformation.

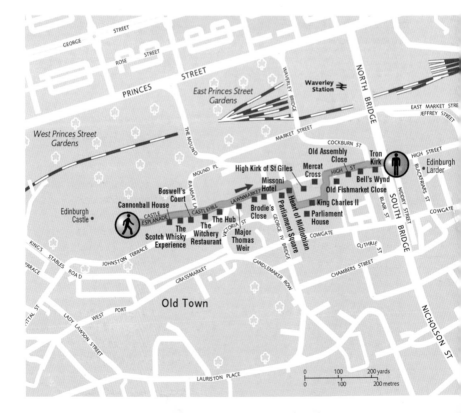

The spot where Deacon Brodie was hanged with the tavern that bears his name beyond

Also on this side of St Giles' you will find **Parliament House**, built between 1632 and 1639. Prior to these dates, the area this building now occupies was the burial ground of St Giles'. Parliament House was the home of the Three Estates – the Lords, Representatives of the Burghs and Representatives of the Country. The voice of the man in the street did not carry much weight so his Member of Parliament spoke for him and acted on his behalf. The Act of Union in 1707 made the function of Parliament House redundant and the hall now accommodates the Court of Session, the Court of Criminal Appeal, the Faculty of Advocates and the National Law Library of Scotland. Inside, the Parliament Hall has an impressive 49-feet wide hammerbeam roof.

He is buried outside at the rear of the church (at one time the location of the graveyard) under what is now parking bay No. 23; if there are no cars do have a look as there is a brass plate inscribed 'I.K. 1572'. There is an excellent café, The Undercroft, beneath St Giles' and this is also well worth a visit for lunch or to sample their home baking.

Also behind St Giles', on the south side, is a statue of **King Charles II** (1630-85) on horseback. It is made of lead and weighs 6 tons. The King is depicted as a Roman General wearing a victor's laurel wreath. The statue was erected before the King's death at a cost of £2,580. It is the oldest equestrian statue in Britain.

Walk around the Cathedral towards the High Street section of the Royal Mile and make your way to the almost circular monument, **The Mercat Cross.** The original Mercat Cross dated from 1365, but this one has a 15th century shaft with later additions. This is where Royal Proclamations were, and still are, announced. Fascinatingly, in this internet and television age, these proclamations are made three days after they are made in London, as it used to take three days for a messenger on horseback to make the journey between the two cities, and the tradition is continued.

Turn right and continue down the Royal Mile where on your right are several interesting closes to explore.

Old Fishmarket Close was also a poultry market. Fish were thrown out on to the street and grabbed by boys and women and sold unwashed from wooden tables exposed to the rain, dust and filth of the city. The last Hangman lived in this close, John Hugh, who died in 1817. He was always easily recognised by his black coat decorated with silver lace and was referred to as the 'man in the magpie coat', for his resemblance to the black and white bird that also has a liking for bright objects. For many years the close was also the home of the Fire Brigade's 'engine' and it would be dragged out on the shout of 'Fire!'.

Old Assembly Close was where the dancing assemblies were held between 1720 and 1766. This was where the ladies and gentlemen of fashionable Edinburgh Society could meet. During the intervals between the dances, oranges were served as refreshment. There was a Mistress of Assemblies who would oversee the whole evening, much like a Master of Ceremonies today.

Just a few steps farther on is **Bell's Wynd** (wynd as in 'eyen-ed' not win-d). This was named after a brewer, John Bell, who lived here in 1529. There were a number of businesses in this close, the Commercial Bank of Scotland, the King's Arms Tavern, the Highland Society and the Children's Shelter. The Wynd also has ghosts said to date back to the murder of Mrs Gourlay and her lover by Mr Gourlay, the jealous husband, many centuries ago. Can you feel their presence?

You will soon be arriving at Hunter Square and the adjoining Blair Street, named after Lord Provost Sir James Hunter Blair, dating from 1786.

Here on the corner of the junction with South Bridge is the **Tron Kirk**. The Tron was the Salt Tron or the old public salt weighing beam that once stood outside the church. If salt merchants sold underweight measures, they were nailed to the weighing beam by their ears, their foot support then kicked away causing their ears to be torn. This meant that people buying salt in the future could tell whether the salt seller was reputable or not.

The church first opened for worship in 1641 and the first minister was John Knox. In 1974 excavations revealed the cobbles of Marlin's Wynd, an ancient roadway, named after the French stonemason John Merlouin who first paved the High Street in 1532.

Traditionally Edinburgh New Year celebrations were held here until the more recent celebrations were introduced in Princes Street.

This walk concludes at the road junction with South Bridge. If you are in need of some sustenance, cross South Bridge and take the second turning on the right. At No.15 Blackfriars Street is the Edinburgh Larder, a delicatessen and licensed cafeteria using delicious seasonal Scottish produce.

Royal Mile part 3

WALK 3

What links Edinburgh to Scotland Yard in London? Find out on this walk which leads on from Walk 1, continuing down the left-hand side of the Royal Mile to the Palace of Holyroodhouse. From the oldest occupied dwelling in the city to the official royal residence, there are many wonderfully historic buildings and closes along the way. Lives of respected poets, a composer, an economist and a courtier are revealed in Canongate Church graveyard and there's a chance for contemplation in a secret 17th-century city garden.

Start	Finish	Distance	Refreshments
High Street – North Bridge junction	Palace of Holyroodhouse	½ mile (1km)	The Story Café; Palace of Holyroodhouse

White Horse Close

ON THIS WALK

	Paisley Close		John Knox House		Canongate Church
		Mowbray House		Canongate Tolbooth	

Begin at the corner of North Bridge and the High Street section of the Royal Mile with your back to the Castle. On your left, you will find one of the oldest closes of the Royal Mile retaining its original name, **Carrubers' Close**, named after William Carrubbers, a merchant who had a mansion here in 1450. John Spottiswood, Lord Chancellor of Scotland and Archbishop of St Andrews, lived here and crowned King Charles I at Holyrood in 1633. In the 1860s it housed the medical dispensary of Sir James Young Simpson (1811-70), who discovered chloroform.

Pass North Gray's Close and Baillie Fyfe's Close. **Paisley Close** is probably one of the most famous closes in the whole of the Royal Mile. It was originally owned by George Henderson who sold the land to Henry Paislie in 1711. This close became infamous on the 24th November 1861 when there was a great disaster. A 250-year old building in the adjacent Baillie Fyfe's Close collapsed, killing 35 residents. While the rescuers were clearing the debris they heard a voice calling, 'Heave awa' lads, ah'm no deid yet!' (Heave away boys, I'm not dead yet!). This was young Joe MacIver trapped in the rubble. When the building was reconstructed, the young lad's face was carved into the lintel above the entrance with a slightly modified inscription of his call for help. As a result of the disaster, the overcrowding and dreadfully cramped living conditions came to the fore and the post of Medical Officer of Health was created.

Chalmers' Close gives access to the Holy Trinity Church Hall. The original Trinity Church was built in the 15th century but was demolished in the 19th century to make way for the railway into Waverley Station. To rebuild the church the stones were carefully labelled and numbered, but so many were stolen to mend walls and make other repairs that there were not enough stones to reconstruct the church, only enough for a hall. The close is named after Patrick Chalmers who was a belt maker and lived in the area.

After Trunks Close, there is an interesting group of buildings, the first being **Mowbray House** which dates from 1630. This is a four-storey house and is the oldest occupied dwelling in Edinburgh. The building survived the burning of the city in 1544 by the Earl of Hertford, who was sent to Scotland by King Henry VIII to 'persuade' the Scottish people to accept a marriage between his son, Edward, then only six, and Mary, daughter of the late James V – eventually Mary Queen of Scots . The marriage did not take place.

Daniel Defoe, the author of *Robinson Crusoe*, lived here in the early 18th century and edited the *Edinburgh Courant* in 1710. He was suspected of being an English government agent in 1707, when the Treaty of Union was

| | Dunbar's Close | | Abbey Strand and Sanctuary | |
| David Rizzio | | White Horse Close | | Palace of Holyroodhouse |

approved, and was pelted with stones and rubbish if he looked out of the windows.

On the pavement in front of Mowbray House is a large stone well, where residents could collect their household water. Next door is the building known as **John Knox House**, dating from 1490, although it originally belonged to James Mossman, the goldsmith to Mary Queen of Scots. His initials, together with that of his wife Mariota Arres, are shown on the outside of the building.

Robert Fergusson

It was said to be the home of John Knox, the church reformer from 1561-1572. The House is open to the public and is part of the Netherbow Arts Centre where the Story Café is located. There are exhibitions on three floors telling of the building's famous inhabitants and their beautiful craftsmanship.

The Centre is named after the Netherbow Port, built in 1513 as the lower gate into the city of Edinburgh. The 17th century bell from the gate is in the Centre. The site of the gate is marked by brass plates in the roadway at the junction outside, marking the boundary between the two burghs of the Canongate and Edinburgh.

Make your way over the road junction and continue down the hill to enter the Canongate section of the Royal Mile. Cross over Cranston Street and New Street. Keep a lookout for a stone-arched doorway with a shield sculpture. This marks **Bible Land** (the word Land refers to the building itself). The other name for the building was Shoemaker's Land. The shield shows an open bible on which is quoted the first verse of the old Scottish version of Psalm 133; the other items shown are a crown and paring knife – symbols of St Crispan, the patron saint of the Canongate shoemakers.

Farther on, come to the **Canongate Tolbooth** in a French chateau style. It dates from 1591 and housed the council chamber and courthouse for the Burgh of the Canongate. The Tolbooth was also a gateway into Edinburgh. Between 1842 and 1848 it was used as an overflow for Calton Jail. There is a wonderful clock overhanging the street which dates from 1879. The building now houses The People's Story, a museum about the lives of the ordinary people of Edinburgh at work and play. There is a wartime kitchen, a jail and a bookbinder's workshop amongst many other interesting artefacts.

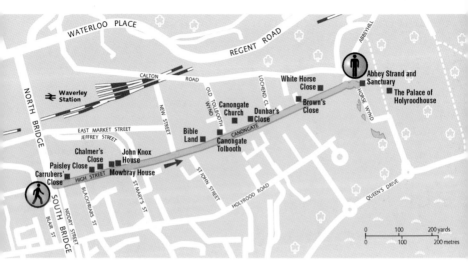

Just past the museum is the **Canongate Church**. It was designed by James Smith in 1688 and built by the Catholic King James VII of Scotland (James II of England) for the congregation from the Abbey Church of Holyrood, when he turned that into a Chapel Royal for the use of the Knights of the Thistle.

On the right side of the gate at the churchyard entrance is the statue of Robert Fergusson (1750-74), a poet. He was born and educated in Edinburgh. Despite having a university degree, he worked as a legal clerk and wrote poems and songs which he performed at private house parties. He could be moody in character and was mentally unwell. He was admitted to the asylum and there had delusions, imagining himself to be a king and he wore a crown of plaited straw. Not long after he took his own life and was buried in a pauper's grave within the Canongate Churchyard. Fergusson admired Robert Burns and Burns thought highly of him, so much so that when he visited Edinburgh in 1787 and found no memorial to Fergusson he saw to it that a suitable gravestone was erected with

the epitaph:
'No sculptured marble here, nor pompous lay
No storied Urn, nor animated Bust;
This simple Stone directs Pale Scotia's way
To pour her Sorrows oe'r her poet's Dust'

Walk to the left of the church and then take the little path on the left to find Fergusson's resting place.

There are a number of other well-known people buried in this graveyard. Just inside the gate and to the left, framed by high black railings, is the resting place of **Adam Smith** (1723-90). He was born at Kirkcaldy, Fife, and is best-known as the father of modern economics. His book *The Wealth of Nations* has had a lasting impact on business people and politicians. He showed how the division of labour could improve productivity and also how value comes from the labour used in production.

Next to Adam Smith is the resting place of **James Gregory** (1753-1821). He was Professor of Medicine at Edinburgh University Medical School and a leading Scottish Consultant. He also produced 'Gregory's mixture' made from magnesia, ginger and rhubarb which, it was said, brought relief for many indigestion sufferers.

Now walk towards the tall steeple-shaped monument near the back of the churchyard. At the path on the left you will find the tomb of **Dugald Stewart** (1753-1828) who was a Professor of Moral Philosophy. He was a superb lecturer and would get up at 3am to walk in his garden to prepare his lectures. He took in students as lodgers, one of them being the future British Prime Minister, Lord Palmerston. If you look up towards Calton Hill you will see the Greek Style temple designed by WH Playfair in 1832 to honour Dugald Stewart.

In the centre of the grassed area is a huge granite edifice decorated with carved crossed muskets and an ammunition belt. This commemorates the soldiers who died whilst on duty at Edinburgh Castle between 1692 and 1880.

Make your way back to the church along the other boundary through the doorway in the wall. Continue up the path towards the largest enclosed grave on the left. En-route you will find the memorial wall-stone to **Johann Frederick Lampe** (1703-51) who was a German musician and composer of 13 operas. He was Handel's favourite bassoonist in London and played at the coronation of King George I. He introduced the idea of open-air concerts in Edinburgh, a tradition which still remains today in Princes Street Gardens.

Walk forward to the boundary wall and turn right to a golden plaque with the delightful profile of a woman. This is a memorial to **Agnes MacElhose** (1759-1841, also known as Nancy Craig) one of the lady friends of the poet, Robert Burns (see Walk 5).

Walk to the wall of the church. Between the first and second window is a flat uneven stone that marks the grave of **David Rizzio** (1533-66). He was born in Turin, Italy, and was recommended to Mary Queen of Scots as a singer for her chapel choir, and later became her private secretary. Mary often confided in Rizzio, much to the consternation of her second husband Lord Darnley. On the 9th March 1566, while Mary was dining with some companions including Rizzio in her Holyrood apartments, Darnley and his armed men came into the room and dragged the Italian away. Rizzio was stabbed 56 times and his body thrown into the Palace courtyard.

Just before you leave the churchyard, if you look to the left you will see the Old Canongate Market Cross which was the main meeting place for traders.

Turn left coming out of the churchyard and walk past a couple of shops to find the entrance to **Dunbar's Close**, a quiet secluded garden, sometimes called The Mushroom Garden and laid out in the style of a 17th century Edinburgh Garden. In 1773 the buildings belonged to writer David Dunbar, hence the close's name. When the poet Robert Burns was in town he would come to Mrs Love's oyster cellar, which was close by, and watch ladies of fashion eating oysters and drinking porter. Take time to relax and enjoy this little garden and imagine the goings on of centuries past.

The next close of note is **Brown's Close or Golfers' Land**. The tenement building known as Golfers' Land stood on this site in the 17th century, built by John Paterson, who made shoes and golf balls. Paterson's bronze coat of arms is shown on the outside of the building. The crest shows a right hand holding a golf club over a knight's helmet. There is also a Latin inscription that reads: 'In the year when Paterson won the prize in golfing, a game peculiar to the Scots, in which his ancestors had nine times won the same honour, he then raised this mansion, a victory more honourable than the rest.'

Near the foot of the Royal Mile you will find **White Horse Close**, appropriately named after Mary Queen of Scot's white palfrey. The close has other royal connections. It was used as the Royal Mews in the 16th century and King Charles I met Scottish nobles here in 1639 for a conference. There was also a hayloft, houses and The White Horse Inn.

The inn was also the terminus for the horse-drawn stage coach service to Newcastle and London. In the 18th century it took the coach eight days to make the journey to London. Scotland Yard in London, home of the Metropolitan Police, got its name because it was the London terminus for the Edinburgh stage coaches. During the Jacobite Rebellion of 1745, the inn was used by the Jacobite officers as their headquarters, while their leader, Prince Charles Edward Stewart, resided in the Palace of Holyroodhouse. The

David Rizzio's gravestone

close also gave its name to a well-known brand of the 'water of life' – whisky.

At the end of the Canongate enter the area known as the **Abbey Strand and Sanctuary**. Many of the old buildings were demolished in the 19th century, but for 300 years, the old medieval right of sanctuary was given to criminals at Holyrood Abbey. The Houses of Refuge were separated from the Canongate by a paved area, the Girth Cross. The right of sanctuary has never been repealed and today there are High Constables of Holyrood who form a guard of honour on ceremonial occasions.

The Palace of Holyroodhouse is well worth a visit, as it is the official residence of the British monarch in Scotland. The site of the palace was originally the guest house for pilgrims to Holyrood Abbey and dates from the 16th century. There is a gift shop and a lovely café in the outer courtyard area.

Royal Mile part 4

WALK 4

This outing follows on from Walk 2 and explores the bottom half of the Royal Mile. Walking towards the Scottish Parliament building, one of the most recent and controversial architectural additions to the city, down the right-hand side of the High Street and Canongate, passing more of the city's ancient past en-route, and presenting you with the opportunity to try one of the country's most talked about delicacies – and it is not haggis.

Start	Finish	Distance	Refreshments
High Street – South Bridge junction	Canongate, at the bottom of the Royal Mile	½ mile (1km)	Clarinda's Tea Room; Scottish Parliament Café

Scottish Parliament

ON THIS WALK

John Logie Baird   Canongate   Moray House

World's End Close   St John's Street

Start this walk at the corner of South Bridge and the High Street section of the Royal Mile by the **Bank Hotel**, built in 1923 as a bank and converted during the 1990s into a Chicago-style speakeasy bar with rooms above. Inside is Logie Baird's Bar, named after **John Logie Baird** (1888-1946), the Scottish inventor and pioneer of television and radio. The bar is themed to famous Scotsmen.

John Logie Baird was the son of a parish minister, born in Helensburgh on the west side of Scotland, not far from Glasgow. He was educated at the Royal Technical College having shown an early inventive bent. He then proceeded to Glasgow University to study for a Bachelor of Science degree. He volunteered for the army in 1914, but was rejected due to his chronic ill-health. He worked as an electrical supply engineer, but is health failed and he set up as a professional inventor.

His early efforts were diverse and unsuccessful. A cure for haemorrhoids was a disaster, as was an attempt to manufacture synthetic diamonds. The Baird Undersock 'for keeping the feet warm in winter and cool in summer' made him a little money, but had some production difficulties. Baird emigrated to Trinidad and then briefly to the United States, but returned to Britain soon after World War I, by which time he was already experimenting with television.

By 1926 he was demonstrating pictures being transmitted from one room to another. Then with the help of the BBC Chief Engineer, he sent pictures along a telephone wire to a BBC studio, which then put them on air with Baird receiving them on his own set 'practically unaltered'. Despite this success, the BBC was fully engaged in the more practical problem of radio and showed no more interest in developing Baird's idea.

In order to succeed he decided to raise money to build his own transmitter and licensed his television station – the first to come into existence. He made technical progress, but his business partners were not seeing a good financial return. Baird became disillusioned and wrote 'If any inventor reads these pages, let him be warned and do what Graham Bell, inventor of the telephone, did and sell for cash. Inventors are no match for financiers'.

He failed to persuade the BBC or the big American radio stations that television was a medium of communication comparable to radio or cinema. He also failed to make money although was offered more than £100,000 for his shares in Baird Television. He was a pure inventor with little business acumen. He continued to develop varieties of television, experimenting with large screen, telephone television, and what he called stereoscopic TV, as well as colour sets. While the mainstream of exploiting

Huntly House		Queensberry House	
Bene's Fish and Chip Shop	Bakehouse Close	Scottish Parliament	

television passed him by, he must be considered the most remarkable innovator of his generation, a man who created the most powerful means of communication in the twentieth century.

Walk down the hill and cross over **Niddry Street.** This used to be the much narrower Niddry Wynd where King James VI and his wife, Anne of Denmark, were helped by Provost Nicol Edward when they were being persecuted by the Earl of Bothwell. In later years the Wynd was home to the Lodge Edinburgh, Mary's Chapel No.1, the oldest authenticated Masonic Lodge in existence.

Cross over **Blackfriars Street,** named after the Blackfriars' Monastery, which was founded by Alexander II in 1230 at the foot of the wynd, but destroyed by riots during the Reformation in 1559.

Next come to **South Gray's Close,** dating from 1512 and named after John Gray. At one time it was Mint Close and Coynehouse Close because it was the home of Scotland's Royal Mint from 1574 until 1877. Part of the old City wall, dating from 1450, is reputed to be part of this close. After this is the **Museum of Childhood** and it's well worth a visit. Admission is free and you can see wonderful toys and games from yesteryear.

The next close on the right is **Tweeddale Court.** Dating from 1589, it was once the home of Sir William Bruce, the architect of more recent parts of Holyrood Palace who died in 1710. His house had a terraced garden and was described by the writer Daniel Defoe as 'one of the most princely buildings in Edinburgh'. In 1806

William Begbie, a porter for the British Linen Company, was stabbed in the close and robbed of a parcel containing £4,392. The Court now houses the Scottish Poetry Library and a sedan chair 'garage'.

A little farther down is **World's End Close,** the last close in the High Street before the old City gate, the Netherbow Port. Its name arose quite literally by being the world's end for many of the local poor. Unless you had money, if you lived in the Canongate you could not afford to enter the walled city and if you lived within the walls you would not be able to afford the return charges. As a result, many residents in Edinburgh lived their entire lives within the city walls. Just after the close you will find The World's End pub – a good spot to eat and drink.

At this corner, if you look left into the roadway, you can see brass plates in amongst the cobbles. This marks the spot where the **Netherbow Port**, old eastern gateway into the city, used to stand; 'port' being another word for a gateway. This was one of six curfew gateways to Edinburgh and was first built in 1513 along with the Flodden Wall, named after the Battle of Flodden which was disastrous for the Scots. King James IV was killed along with many in his army. The gatehouse was demolished in 1764.

Continue over St Mary's Street to move into the Canongate section of the Royal Mile. The **Canongate** was founded in 1128 by King David I, who granted the Augustinian monks of the Castle the right to establish a burgh on the waste ground between Calton Hill and Arthur's Seat. Canongate derives from

'Canongait', which means the 'way or street of the canons'. Before the 18th century the Canongate had many illustrious residents: sixteen earls, two countesses, two dukes, seven lords, thirteen baronets, seven lords of session and four commanders-in-chief.

Pass **Gullan's Close** and then come to some archways leading into **Chessel's Court**. This court has some of the finest examples of mansion flats and apartments in the Old Town, built in 1748 by Archibald Chessel, a merchant. There was a hotel here in 1781-83, Clark's Hotel, the first in the Old Town 'for the Reception of the Nobility and Gentry'. The close achieved notoriety in 1788 when Deacon William Brodie burgled the excise office, but he was caught and later hanged for this and other offences (see Walks 1 and 2). The buildings were fully restored in 1963.

Just past Chessel's Court is **Old Playhouse Close,** which led to the first of Edinburgh's theatres. The Canongate Theatre was founded in 1746 by John Ryan, an actor from London's Covent Garden. Many famous actors and singers entertained here up until 1786. Just below this close a Maltese Cross was painted on the roadway to mark the boundary between Edinburgh and the Burgh of Canongate.

St John's Street is the next close where the Knights of St John had their house, which was built around 1768. Robert Burns was made Poet Laureate in Freemasons' Lodge Canongate Kilwinning No.2 in 1787. The land belonged to many religious groups subject to the Canons of Holyrood. The Knights were from landowning families who built homes close to the Palace. The Priory of Scotland of the Most Venerable Order of St John still exists today and is mainly concerned with charitable fund raising. A Maltese Cross can be seen on the gate and above the doorway.

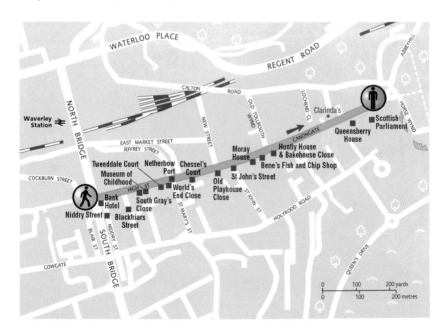

Tobias Smollett lived here in his sister's house in 1766 while writing his book *Humphrey Clinker*. This extract from the book gives an idea of what living was like in such a house in the 18th century: 'We are settled in convenient lodgings, up four pairs of stairs in the High Street, the fourth storey being, in this city, reckoned more genteel than the first. Every storey is a complete house, occupied by a separate family; the stair being common to them all is generally left in a very filthy condition: a man must tread with great circumspection to get safe housed with unpolluted shoes.'

The large building on the right with a balcony overhanging the street is **Moray House**, built in 1625 it is one of the finest mansions to survive in the Old Town. Moray House was built by Mary, Dowager Countess of Home. Oliver Cromwell stayed here in 1648 and made it his headquarters. The Treaty of Union between Scotland and England was signed here in 1707. The building is now Moray House College of Education, a teacher training school.

If you are feeling hungry you may be tempted by **Bene's Fish and Chip Shop**, where you'll find deep fried Mars Bar on the menu. Not for the faint hearted, but world famous, so if you wish to try it, now is your chance! Alternatively you can try traditional fish and chips or haggis.

Continue down Canongate to reach **Huntly House.** This building dates from 1570 and is sometimes referred to as The Speaking House because of the series of Latin inscriptions on the facade. The originals are inside in the museum but an extra one was added in 1932 – ANTI QUA TAMEN JUVEN ESCO – 'However old, I am getting younger'.

This was the home of the Dowager Countess of Gordon. There were three houses on this site in 1517 but they were knocked through in 1570 and extended into the street. The house was saved by Edinburgh Corporation in 1926 and restored as the Museum of Edinburgh. It contains many interesting objects including Greyfriars Bobby's collar and dish (see Walk 6).

Huntly House also incorporates **Bakehouse Close**, formerly known as Huntly Close or Hammermen's Close, as it was the site of the Headquarters of the Hammermen. The Hammermen were tradesmen,

Canongate Tolbooth clock

the equivalent today being engineers, and the Incorporation of Hammermen was formed circa 1477.

The close gave access to every part of the house as there was no direct opening on to the street, thus providing extra security when the gate was shut. The current name comes from the bakehouse and property on the west side which was occupied by the Guild of the Incorporation of Bakers of the Canongate in 1832. It was also the home of the Acheson family who provided the household staff of Kings James VI and Charles I. Records show that in 1851, 230 people lived within this close.

Clarinda's Tea Room

Wander down to the large cream-coloured building, **Queensberry House**. It dates from 1681 and was eventually bought by William, 1st Duke of Queensberry; and it holds a terrible footnote straight out of a 'horrible history'. The Duke's eldest grandson, Lord Drumlanrig, was known to be insane, so was kept hidden and locked up in a room in the house. On the night of the signing of the Treaty of Union in 1707, while his father and servants were out, Lord Drumlanrig felt hungry and escaped from his room to look for food. Unfortunately, all he could find was a kitchen boy. His father returned to catch him roasting and eating the flesh of the poor lad. Later, the building was a barracks in the 19th century, then a 'House of Refuge for the Destitute' and a Hospital for the Elderly. It has now been incorporated into the Scottish Parliament Building.

You are now approaching the end of the Royal Mile and one of the most modern, and controversial buildings in Scotland, let alone Edinburgh.

The **Scottish Parliament** building was designed by a Catalonian architect, Enric Miralles. It has been the home of the Scottish Government since September 2004 and was officially opened by Her Majesty the Queen on 9th October 2004. It was thought the construction would cost around £40 million but, in the final reckoning, the bill was closer to £414 million. It is said that the inspiration for the design was from the upturned fishing boats on the shore and from leaf shapes. The construction uses many Scottish materials such as granite from Aberdeenshire, stone from Caithness and sycamore and oak wood along with steel and glass. There is even a grassed roof area, but roof tiles from Queensberry House have also been used. The Canongate Wall, the side facing the Royal Mile has many Scottish carved stones incorporated into the building. The Scottish Parliament is open to the public for guided tours and there is a cafeteria and shop.

Try Clarinda's Tea Room in Canongate or the cafeteria in the Scottish Parliament.

Calton Hill and Old Calton Graveyard

WALK 5

This is a walk of diverse characters, encountering a pioneering African adventurer, one of Scotland's most celebrated novelists and its most famous poet, the Iron Duke and an American president, all on the way to what must be regarded as the best-known view over Edinburgh.

Start	Finish	Distance	Refreshments
Waverley Bridge – Princes Street junction	Waterloo Place – Leith Street junction	2 miles (3.4km)	Balmoral Hotel; The Café Royal

Old Calton Graveyard

ON THIS WALK

Sir Walter Scott Monument	Balmoral Hotel	Old Calton Burial Ground
Dr David Livingstone	Register House	

Begin at the junction of Princes Street and Waverley Bridge, where the mainline railway arrives in the city. Trains have been running here since June 1846. The name Waverley comes from the 'The Waverley Novels' by Sir Walter Scott. There used to be a green or vegetable market where the station now stands.

Catching the eye here is a huge monument with statues all around the outside on many levels. This is the **Sir Walter Scott Monument**. Scott (1771-1832) was one of Scotland's greatest writers; two of his more well-known books are *Rob Roy* and *Ivanhoe*. The monument's foundation stone was laid on the 15th August 1840, which would have been Scott's 69th birthday. The day was made a public holiday. The monument is just over 200 feet high and the foundations lie 52 feet deep under the Princes Street Gardens. Charles Dickens, who often visited Edinburgh, believed it was a failure and said 'It is like the spire of a Gothic church taken off and stuck in the ground!' At the base of the monument you can see a Carrara marble statue of Scott with his faithful deerhound, Maida. If you are feeling energetic you can make your way up the small staircase within the monument to get right to the top and see amazing views over the city.

Beside the Scott Monument is a statue of **Dr David Livingstone** (1813-73), the Victorian missionary and explorer. He was born at Blantyre, close to Glasgow. Although his schooling ended when he was ten years old he loved to read and developed a keen interest in nature and science, even when working in the local cotton mill. He studied medicine and also became a trainee missionary with the London Missionary Society. He went to Africa in 1841. At that time it was referred to as the Dark Continent because so little was known of the African interior. He covered 30,000 square miles during the course of his missionary work. In 1871 his health was deteriorating when he was visited by the journalist Morton Stanley, who uttered those now famous words 'Dr Livingstone, I presume?'

Livingstone was disgusted by the slave trade, campaigning against it during his time in Africa. On his final journey of exploration in the region now covered by Zambia he became very ill and passed away. His faithful followers carried his body for 1,500 miles to the coast and his remains were brought back to Britain to be buried in Westminster Abbey, London.

Walk to the right along Princes Street towards the large building with the prominent clock tower. This is the **Balmoral Hotel**, once the Station Hotel, and the clock is always kept a few minutes fast to help people not miss their trains. The author JK Rowling finished the Harry Potter series of books here in Room 652 on the 11th January 2007.

Nelson Monument

Whisky Row

Calton Hill

Burns Monument

The Café Royal

Once outside the Balmoral Hotel look cross the road towards the building with the statue of a horseman at the front. This magnificent gold sandstone building is **Register House**, the oldest purpose-built home of any national archive in Europe. It was designed in 1771 by Robert Adam. If you want to trace your Scottish ancestry, this is the place to start as it houses the birth, wedding and death ('hatch, match and despatch') certificates.

The large statue is the **Duke of Wellington** (1769-1852) on his horse, Copenhagen. The statue weighs 12 tons and was towed by 30 men and 8 horses into position on 18th June 1849, on the anniversary of the Battle of Waterloo (1815). The Duke of Wellington was nicknamed 'The Iron Duke' because he had iron shutters installed on his London home to protect the windows during riots. This statue was designed by Sir John Steell and is referred to as 'the iron duke, cast in bronze by a man named Steell'

Duke of Wellington

Keep walking past the Balmoral Hotel and cross North Bridge at the pedestrian crossing. Continue past the large building on your right, once the Theatre Royal and then the General Post Office, and walk past the bus stops along Waterloo Place. Nearing the far end of the bus stops, take the entrance on your right into the **Old Calton Burial Ground**.

As you get to the top of the entrance steps you will see a huge pointed stone obelisk. This is the Political Martyrs Monument to those who fought for electoral reform in the 18th century.

On the main path towards the obelisk, notice over to the right the statue of a very well-known American gentleman. His stance is a tell-tale sign of his identity. It is the life-size figure of President **Abraham Lincoln**, freeing the slave who sits below him with

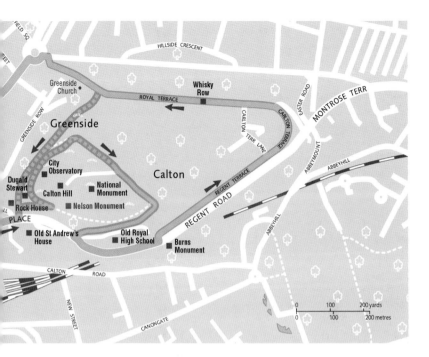

the battle flags. This monument also marks the graves of five Scotsmen who died in the American Civil War of 1861-65. Sergeant Major John McEwan of the 65th Illinois Volunteer Rifles; Lieutenant Colonel William Duff of the 2nd Illinois Artillery; Robert Steedman of the 5th Maine Infantry Volunteers; James Wilkie of the 1st Michigan Cavalry and Robert Ferguson of the 57th New York Infantry Volunteers. A part of America right in the heart of the city of Edinburgh.

To the left of Abraham Lincoln is a huge cylindrical monument with a large urn on the front. This monument marks the resting place of **David Hume** (1711-76). David Hume was an eminent Scottish philosopher and a leading figure in the history of Western philosophy. He was born in Edinburgh and studied law at the university, and published many essays and books. There were rumours that he made a pact with the Devil; these were taken so seriously

by some of his friends that they kept a watch over his tomb every evening for eight nights after the funeral.

At the back of the Hume Monument is the unmarked wall grave of the sculptor Sir John Steell (1804-91). It has a black mortsafe, designed to protect the grave from body-snatchers.

Now retrace your route out of the graveyard, down the steps and turn right. A few yards along the road you will come to a large Art Deco style building, **Old St Andrew's House**, which was built in the 1930s and was opened the day after war was declared in 1939. It was the principal seat of the Scottish Office and now houses the executive offices of the Scottish Government.

Cross the road and climb a set of steps taking you up on to the top of **Calton Hill**. It is the remnant of a long-extinct volcano. At the summit, the park offers outstanding views over the city.

There are a number of monuments and buildings at the top of Calton Hill. The one that looks like a huge upturned telescope is, quite appropriately, the **Nelson Monument** to Lord Horatio Nelson. A mast 30 feet tall on the top has a time-ball that falls when the one o' clock gun is fired from Edinburgh Castle. The time-ball was installed in 1852 to act as a signal to ships to set their chronometers. On the 21st October, Trafalgar Day, the monument displays flags that read 'England expects every man to do his duty', Nelson's famous command signalled at the Battle of Trafalgar in 1805.

The building behind the wall is the **City Observatory** which was founded in 1818 as the New Observatory of the Astronomical Institution of Edinburgh. It is based on the Greek Temple of the Winds. It is no longer in use.

There is a row of 12 very large pillars and some steps to your right; this is the **National Monument**, commemorating the fallen of the Napoleonic Wars. The foundation stone was laid in 1822 by King George IV and it was to be a copy of the Parthenon, the temple of the goddess Athena on the hill of the Acropolis in Athens. It was intended to form a Hall of Heroes with statues of the greatest Scottish men and women, but the project was never completed, only half of the £42,000 was raised from the citizens of the city and it became known as 'Edinburgh's Folly' and 'Edinburgh's Disgrace'.

Enjoy a short circuit around the top of the hill in a clockwise direction. Walk first towards a cylindrical pillared monument dedicated to the memory of **Dugald Stewart** (1753-1828), a professor of Moral Philosophy at Edinburgh University. It is based on the Choragic Monument of Lysicrates in Athens.

As you walk towards this on the narrow path around the top of the hill, there is on your right a curious little house built directly out of the rock, appropriately called Rock House. It was the home and studio of David Octavius Hill who was a 19th century pioneering photographer. From this point you have panoramic views over the city.

Continue around this path then leave the hill by the wider roadway, the National Monument will be on your right as you make your way down the hill. The dark green shrub with thorns, and possibly some bright yellow flowers, lining the slope as you go down is called gorse. There's a saying in Scotland that 'when the gorse is in bloom, it is the kissing time' and Scots are very lucky because it blooms all year long.

When you arrive at the foot of the hill go through the gated opening and turn left, passing the entrance to New Parliament House. This building is the **Old Royal High School** built 1825-29. The design style of this building is termed 'Scottish Greek Revival'; you can see how Edinburgh gets the name 'The Athens of the North'. It is now offices.

Continue along the left-hand side of Regent Road. Shortly, on the opposite side you will see the **Burns Monument**. Built by architect Thomas Hamilton in 1830, it is a variation of the

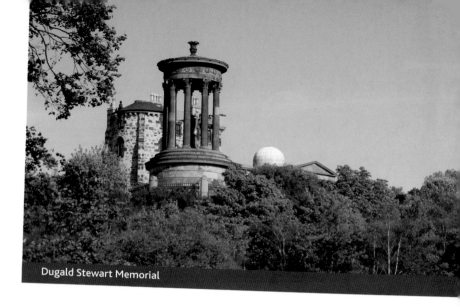
Dugald Stewart Memorial

one at Alloway, Ayrshire, the birthplace of the celebrated poet Robert Burns (1759-96). The monument overlooks Canongate Graveyard where one of his lady friends, Agnes MacElhose, has her final resting place. They wrote love letters to each other and Robert signed his name as 'Sylvander', Agnes signed hers as 'Clarinda', to protect their identities. He wrote his poem 'Ae fond kiss' for her:

'Ae fond kiss, and then we sever!
Ae farewell, and then forever!
Deep in heart-wrung tears I'll pledge thee,
Warring sighs and groans I'll wage thee.'

Turn left into **Regent Terrace**. At number 3 is the office of the Consulate of the United States; you may see the flag of the 'stars and stripes' flying above your head. Regent Terrace was designed by William Playfair and built between 1819 and 1860. Follow it round to the left when it becomes Carlton Terrace and then Royal Terrace. Known by the nickname **Whisky Row**, Royal Terrace was given this title when whisky merchants had their

Edinburgh town houses here.

Near the bottom of the slope towards the end of Royal Terrace, before Greenside church, there's a path off to the left taking you back to Calton Hill. Take this to conclude the walk in energetic fashion, over the hill to reach Waterloo Place. Alternatively, continue along Royal Terrace to Leith Street, a major road junction, keeping to the left-hand side, going past the Playhouse Theatre and the modern Omni Centre to return to the junction of Princes Street and Waterloo Place.

Try the Balmoral Hotel for afternoon tea or to dine in their restaurant where Ian Rankin's Inspector Rebus wined and dined a lady client. Or you may prefer **The Café Royal** bar and restaurant, a listed building dating from 1861, which has beautiful Victorian plasterwork, stained glass and irreplaceable ceramic Doulton murals. It is located at the end of West Register Street, found by turning right beyond Register House.

Grassmarket and Greyfriars

WALK 6

The sordid world of the Resurrectionists, the charming tale of a faithful four-legged friend and the early years of a very well-known Hollywood screen legend conspire to make a fascinating walk through this part of Edinburgh's Old Town. You may be able to sense the inspiration from the window in the Elephant House where JK Rowling started her writing, but the stories of Maggie Dickson and James Barry are much stranger than any fiction and just as amazing.

Start	Finish	Distance	Refreshments
Princes Street – Lothian Road junction	Candlemaker Row	1½ miles (2.3km)	The Elephant House; Greyfriars Bobby's Bar

Greyfriars Bobby

ON THIS WALK

St Cuthbert's graveyard	Burke and Hare	Maggie Dickson's
James Bond	Grassmarket	

Start at the west end of Princes Street at the junction with Lothian Road. Face **St John's Episcopal Church** designed by William Burn in 1815-18. This church has the finest collection of Victorian stained glass in Scotland.

Walk up the left-hand side of Lothian Road past the church.

Its adjoining graveyard is the final resting place of Anne Rutherford, the mother of Sir Walter Scott, and Sir Henry Raeburn, the artist. Shortly, come to a corner with a small circular building on your left in the neighbouring **St Cuthbert's graveyard**. This graveyard was an easy target for body-snatchers or, as they preferred to be called, 'Resurrectionists'. The circular building was a watchtower where an appointed officer kept death records and watched over the burial ground in case corpse-stealers should come by. Stolen bodies would have been sold to the Edinburgh Medical School for dissection, £10 for a male body and £8 for a female one.

Take the second left, Castle Terrace. To the left sits **Edinburgh Castle** atop its craggy, volcanic perch. During the last Ice Age, a vast sheet of ice moving west to east scooped away the soft ground exposing this outcrop of an ancient volcanic plug.

On your right is a large modern sandstone office building, Saltire Court, built in 1991. The site was originally destined for an Opera House but this never came to fruition.

Continue to the road junction and there dog-leg right and then left into Lady Lawson Street. Keep ahead at the crossroads. Just a few paces up on the left-hand side is the entrance to **Edinburgh College of Art.** In the early 1950s, Tommy Connery was a regular model in the life drawing classes here, showing off the muscles he had built up attending a weight-lifting club. Later, this young man changed his name to Sean Connery and became best-known for his role as James Bond, 007.

Make your way back down the hill to the crossroads and turn right into West Port. **The West Port** was one of the gates in the old Flodden Wall, which was built between 1513 and 1560, after the Battle of Flodden, to protect the city. At one time the West Port was a trading area for the produce from local orchards and gardens, but it was also the gateway where the severed heads of low-ranking criminals were spiked. In 1689, John Graham of Claverhouse, Viscount Dundee, rode out of the West Port at the front of 60 cavaliers, taking the road north to raise an army in the Highlands. This event is commemorated in a Scottish song:

'Unhook the West Port
And let us gae free

	The Elephant House	Greyfriars churchyard	
National Library of Scotland	Greyfriars Bobby	'James' Miranda Barry	

The Elephant House

For it's up wi' the bonnets
O'Bonnie Dundee'

This area was also home to two infamous figures in 19th century Edinburgh, William Burke (1792-1829) and William Hare (1804-1860), the notorious **Burke and Hare**. In the late 1820s, a fall in the number of criminal executions deprived Edinburgh Medical School of its only legal source of cadavers. Burke and Hare, originally from Ulster in Ireland, realised that money could be made by selling bodies to the Medical School for dissection. Rather than body-snatching from local graveyards, they schemed to encourage potential victims to their lodgings in the West Port. There Burke and Hare plied them with whisky, suffocated them without leaving any obvious trace of death, and sold the bodies to Dr Knox at the Medical School. They committed 16 murders before being arrested.

As there was not overwhelming evidence against the pair, Hare was offered a guarantee against prosecution if he confessed and testified against Burke. He took this offer and sent his colleague to the gallows. Burke was duly hanged and his body went for

public dissection at the Medical School. Hare fled Scotland and died a pauper in London.

Continue down to the foot of West Port to arrive at an open, rectangular area called Grassmarket. This was the livestock and corn market in the 16th and 18th centuries. It is now a lively part of town with many fine pubs, cafés and small shops; but at one time it was a site for public hangings. Walk straight ahead to the far end of Grassmarket. The gallows was located here, in the middle of this area. To the left are a couple of interesting pubs: The Last Drop – either the last drop of drink in your glass or the last drop before the trap door in the gallows opens and the hangman's noose tightens – and **Maggie Dickson's**.

Margaret Dickson was hanged here having been found guilty of murdering

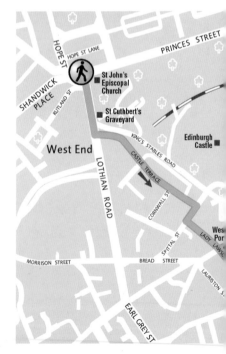

her illegitimate baby. Her body was declared dead, taken from the scaffold and put in a coffin on the back of a cart to go for burial. But as the cart driver was trundling through the streets he heard a knocking noise and a muffled voice saying 'let me out, let me out, my neck is sore!' This was poor Maggie, very much alive. As she had been declared dead by the magistrate, she was not retried and went on to live a long life bearing many more children. She did get the title of 'Half hangit Maggie' and her memory lives on in the name of the pub.

Turn left and make your way up the curved slope of Victoria Street, with its quaint shops and pedestrian terrace above, to reach the main road junction with George IV Bridge. Turn right. On the opposite side of the road you will see the **National Library of Scotland**, built in the 1930s. It houses many rare books and often has an interesting exhibition. The Moir Rare Book Collection is one of the very finest consisting of 250 volumes of rare beekeeping books, some of which were published as far back as 1525. The library also houses a collection of Post Office directories dating from 1773 to 1911, which give a wonderful insight into the trades, families and history of Scotland.

Keep to the right-hand side of George IV Bridge to find the Edinburgh Central Lending Library which was built in 1887. It is worth going inside to see the splendid interior and grand staircase.

Farther along, come to **The Elephant House**. Do go into this lovely café and partake of some refreshments. Try and find the table through in the back room with the large window and marvel at the view.

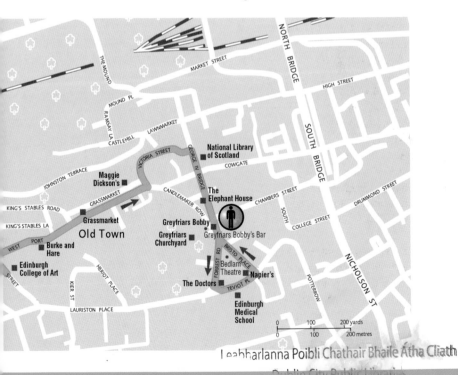

This is where JK Rowling sat and started writing the Harry Potter series. Can you feel the inspiration as you look over the buildings of the Old Town?

Keep ahead along George IV Bridge to find Edinburgh's most famous statue, a little dog by the name of Greyfriars Bobby. The bronze statue is on top of a drinking fountain, the lower part being for dogs. Bobby was a Skye terrier who befriended a man called John Gray. They went everywhere together and each day, on the stroke of one o' clock, (a time gun was and is still fired at the castle) would take their lunch in Mr Traill's Refreshment Rooms. One very severe winter John Gray took ill and passed away, to be buried in the churchyard behind the buildings where you are now standing. Bobby was so upset by this he sat on is master's grave for 14 years and during this time he was still fed every day by Mr Traill. When Bobby died in 1858, he too was given his own spot in the churchyard.

From the statue you can see Greyfriars Bobby's Bar and to the right of it is the Candlemaker's Hall, which was built in 1722 and was the Guildhall of the Corporation of Candlemakers. This lies on Candlemaker Row which leads back to the Grassmarket.

To the left of Bobby's Bar is the entrance to **Greyfriars Churchyard. Enter the churchyard.** You are standing on the site of the old monastery of the Franciscan Brothers who wore brown habits; in those days brown was classed as a shade of grey, hence the name Greyfriars. The Franciscan monks came to Edinburgh in 1447 as medical missionaries to the poor and sick.

The pink granite gravestone in front of you was erected in 1981 by the Dog Aid Society in memory of the faithful little Skye terrier who became known as Greyfriars Bobby. If you walk to the right down the narrow path, after a few paces you will find the final resting place of Bobby's master, John Gray (1838-58) on your left.

There are many famous people buried in this graveyard but Greyfriars was also the setting for the signing of the National Covenant in 1638. The Covenant was a protest by Scottish Presbyterians against the new English forms of worship introduced by King Charles I. If you continue down this path you will come to the Martyrs Monument, with its large triangular pediment on top and the text of a long prayer dedicated to the Covenanters, those who fought for this cause. One thousand two hundred Covenanters were held prisoner in the churchyard for five months in the open with no shelter and little food. Many were eventually transported to plantations in the West Indies, some were executed and a few released if they promised not to rebel, but more than a hundred are buried close to this monument.

Upon leaving the churchyard turn right and walk up Forrest Road. On the opposite side of the road there is a church which now is home to the Bedlam Theatre, so named because the church is on the site of the old sanatorium.

Keep going up Forrest Road and cross at the junction to find yourself standing at a pub called The Doctors. The pub is appropriately named because the large building opposite is the Edinburgh

Napier's the herbalist

Medical School and the pub has been a social meeting place for medical students for many years. One of the most interesting doctors to graduate from the Medical School was James Barry. 'James' Miranda Stuart Barry (1790-1865) lived in the days when a career in medicine was forbidden to women. She worked her way through to the highest rank in the British Army Medical Service disguised as a man, even serving in the Crimean War. Her main concern was the soldiers' diets and living conditions and in 1857 she became Inspector General of Military Hospitals in Montreal and Quebec, successfully concealing her gender up until her death in London in 1865.

Inside the Doctors there are many photographs and historical artefacts with associations to the medical profession.

Now walk along Teviot Place past the pub, the **Edinburgh Medical School**, which was completed in 1888, on your right. Look at the two black lamp posts on either side of the entrance to the Medical School. At the base of the lamps are creatures that resemble dolphins, but are actually leeches. Medically, leeches were used widely in years gone being regarded as something of a panacea; and they are making a come-back today in alternative medicine.

Look into the arcade entrance at the many plaques to notable Medical School graduates including Sir James Young Simpson (1811-70), who discovered chloroform and Sophia Jex-Blake (1840-1912), a pioneer of medical education for women and founder of the Edinburgh Hospital for Women and Children.

As you continue along the street there are university buildings on your right in an area known as Potter Row (named long before Harry Potter's creation). On the corner with Bristo Place, on the left, is **Napier's the Herbalist**, founded by Duncan Napier, an eminent Victorian herbalist and botanist, on the 25th May 1860 and it continues to provide healthcare products today.

Turn left at Napier's and this will lead you back towards the Bedlam Theatre. You can then retrace your steps to enjoy refreshments at The Elephant House, Greyfriars Bobby's Bar or walk down Candlemaker Row back to the pubs in the Grassmarket.

Georgian New Town

WALK 7

By the 18th century the population of the city was growing fast and the Old Town was very overcrowded. In 1767 a competition was held to design a New Town. The winner was James Craig (1744-95), whose plan was to create three main, parallel streets (Princes Street, George Street and Queen Street), with a grand square at each end. It was called the Georgian New Town after the reigning monarch King George III.

Start	Finish	Distance	Refreshments
Princes Street – The Mound junction	The Oxford Bar, Young Street	2¾ miles (4.7km)	The Dome; The Oxford Bar

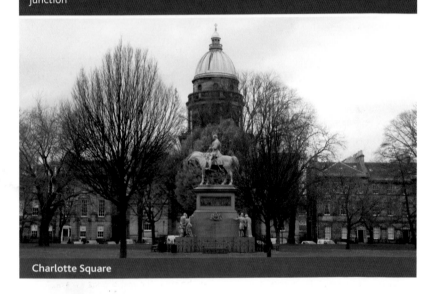

Charlotte Square

ON THIS WALK

The Mound — Alexander Graham Bell — Sir James Young Simpson

The Floral Clock — The Georgian House

Begin at the foot of The Mound, halfway along Princes Street. **The Mound** was created from over two million cartloads of earth dug from the foundations of the New Town. The gardens on your left are also a New Town creation. They lie on the site of Nor Loch, an artificial defensive lake created below the castle in 1460. Eels and trout were a delicacy in the local taverns. The loch was the scene of witchcraft trials. Supposed witches were tied to a ducking stool and plunged into the water: if they drowned they were innocent, if they survived they were taken up to Castlehill and burnt at the stake.

The statue ahead is of **Allan Ramsay** (1686-1758) who started the first circulating library in Scotland. He lived in Ramsay Gardens in a house known today as Ramsay Lodge, the white buildings seen up to the left of the castle.

Just below Ramsay's statue there is a flight of steps leading to **The Floral Clock**. Created in 1904, the mechanism lies in the plinth base of Ramsay's statue. The clock is 36 feet wide and the hands are 8 feet and 5 feet long. The clock is made with 24,000 plants and a mechanical cuckoo pops out of the small bird house above the clock face each quarter-hour.

Walk along Princes Street with the gardens and an excellent view of the castle to the left.

The bronze monument of a trooper on horseback standing on a rock commemorates members of the **Royal Scots Greys Regiment** who died in the Boer War (1899-1902). At the time of the Boer War the regiment's Colonel-in-Chief appointed by Queen Victoria was the Russian Emperor, Tsar Nicholas II.

Just prior to St John's Episcopal Church on the left, cross Princes Street into South Charlotte Street. Cross to the left-hand side of the street to find the home of **Alexander Graham Bell** (1847-1922), the inventor of the telephone. There is a plaque by the door. He eventually moved to the United States where he taught deaf children by day and experimented with telecommunications by night. The first telephone call was to his assistant – 'Come here, Mr Watson, I want to see you.'

Pass Bell's house into **Charlotte Square**, named after Queen Charlotte, the wife of George III. The square was planned by Robert Adam in 1791, with symmetrical sides and each 'palace front' has 11 individual three-storey houses. Almost all of these dwellings are now offices.

Go around the square keeping to the left. In the middle of the grass covered square is a large statue of **Prince Albert** (1819-61), consort and husband to Queen Victoria. John Steell was the sculptor and the statue was

Robert Louis Stevenson		The Melville Monument	
Heriot Row	The Conan Doyle		Daylight robbery

unveiled by Queen Victoria on 17th August 1876.

On the west side of this magnificent square is **West Register House**, originally St George's Church in 18th century Edinburgh. The building was modified in 1971 to provide more space for historical documents.

On the north side of the square, there's a plaque to the surgeon **Joseph Lister** (1827-1912) who lived for some time in this square. He developed a spray for disinfecting hospital operating theatres and became famous for pioneering antiseptic surgery.

At No.7 Charlotte Square is **The Georgian House**. A visit behind these doors is a trip back in time as the house is exactly as it was when first occupied in the 18th century. It is open to the public and offers a fascinating insight into the life of a respectable Georgian Edinburgh family.

Next door is **Bute House**, the official residence of the first minister of the Scottish Parliament.

Turn left upon reaching North Charlotte Street and walk down the hill.

If you are a Rebus fan and/or in need of refreshment, make a quick detour across the road into the narrow Young Street. A few paces along on the right-hand side you will find the **Oxford Bar**, a favourite of Ian Rankin, author and creator of the Rebus stories.

At the bottom of North Charlotte Street, you will come to a monument dedicated to the author

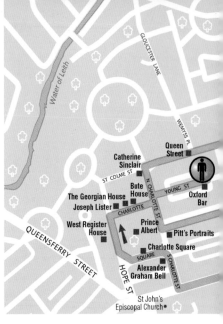

and benefactor **Catherine Sinclair** (1800-64). She started a school to teach young girls about domestic service, gave pensions to the elderly and opened kitchens where the poor could get soup, bread and potatoes.

Use the pedestrian crossing to turn right into **Queen Street** keeping on the right-hand side. Also named after Queen Charlotte of Mecklenburg Strelitz, wife of George III, it was designed to this width to accommodate the turning circle of a carriage and four horses.

Just up North Castle Street, on the left at No. 39, was the Edinburgh town house of **Sir Walter Scott**, prior to his move to the Scottish Borders.

Keep ahead along Queen Street. **Sir James Young Simpson** (1811-70) lived at No. 52. He entered Edinburgh University at the age of 14 and later became a physician. As Professor of Midwifery, in 1835, he conducted research into an anaesthetic to ease the pain of childbirth. He tested chloroform on himself and his friends at dinner

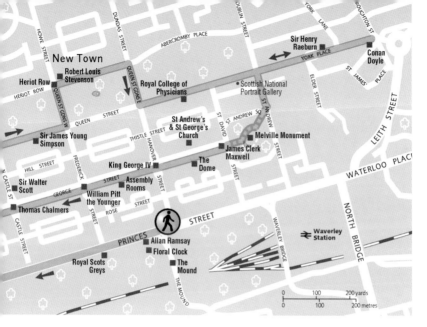

New Town

parties and they would all end up unconscious under the dining table. He was one of Queen Victoria's physicians when she was in Scotland and criticism of his anaesthetic was silenced when Prince Leopold was born in 1853 after chloroform was administered to the Queen.

At the next corner, the junction with Frederick Street, cross Queen Street and walk down Queen Street Gardens West. St Stephen's Church lies ahead. Pause on the next corner. **Heriot Row** is one of the most desirable addresses in Edinburgh. Most of the houses were built in 1808, good sized family homes, but smaller than the grand ones in Charlotte Square. Now a charming, quiet street, it has not always been so peaceful. In 1814 the Grant family moved into No. 4. Elizabeth Grant wrote her memoirs and describes a riot at the house in 1815: '...a large party with dancing, food, card playing and music all in separate rooms. Such was the noise that they were unaware that a rioting mob was outside. The first indications were when a shower of

stones came through the windows and several ladies fainted'.

At this point cross Queens Street Gardens West, then cross again to the other side of Heriot Row. The houses will be on your left and the gardens opposite.

Between 1856 and 1880, No.17 was the home of **Robert Louis Stevenson** (1850-94), the author of *Kidnapped* and *Dr Jekyll and Mr Hyde*. He was a very sickly child and spent much of his time in his bed. As you look at the house, his bedroom was on the level above the front door so he could look down on the street below. The lamps in this street, now all electric, used to be lit by hand by a lamplighter. In Edinburgh the lamplighter was known as 'Leerie'. The young Robert would look out on this scene as darkness fell and later it inspired his poem *The Lamplighter* describing this early evening event:

'For we are very lucky, with a lamp
before the door
And Leerie stops to light it as he
lights so many more
And O! before you hurry by with

ladder and with light
O Leerie see a little boy and nod to
him tonight'

Outside No.17 at the base of the lamp
you will see a brass plate inscribed with
these four lines.

Across from the houses are gardens
which are for the private use of the
residents in the street. It is said that
when Robert was a young boy he
played in these gardens and in those
days there was a pond with and island
in the middle, which inspired him in
later life to write his most famous book,
Treasure Island. It is hard to imagine
that Long John Silver and the 'pieces of
eight' started life in this quiet Georgian
Edinburgh Street.

At the next road junction, go
right into Queen Street Gardens
East and walk up the hill. On
meeting Queen Street turn
left, once again keeping to the
left-hand side. Soon, on your right,
you will see a building with pillars and
decorative lamps and statues. This is
the **Royal College of Physicians**, given
a Royal Charter by King Charles II in
1681. The building was designed by
Thomas Hamilton in 1845. The statues
are of Aesculapius, God of Medicine,
and Hippocrates, the 'first' physician
and representation of Hygeia, Goddess
of Healing.

Keep straight on and, beyond
the splendid pinkish-red
sandstone building of the
Scottish National Portrait
Gallery, pass into York Place. On
the left at No. 32, above a window, you
will see an artist's palate carved in the
stonework. This marks the studio of
Sir Henry Raeburn (1756-1823), the

Robert Louis Stevenson's house

famous portrait painter. You can see
many of his works in the galleries in the
city, one of the more well-known being
*The Reverend Robert Walker Skating on
Duddingston Loch* (see Walk 15).

Upon reaching St Paul and St
George's Church on the corner
with Broughton Street, cross to
the **Conan Doyle** pub. Sir Arthur
Conan Doyle (1859-1930) lived in this
part of Edinburgh. He studied medicine,
but he was also a great writer. One of
his teachers was Dr Joseph Bell, whom
Doyle admired hugely for his enquiring
mind. Sherlock Holmes, Doyle's great
detective, was based on Dr Bell. You can
see a statue of Mr Holmes resplendent
in his tweed cape and deerstalker hat,
located in the small group of trees
diagonally across from the pub.

Now, with the pub on your left,
make your way back along York
Place. Approaching The Scottish
National Portrait Gallery turn
left up North St Andrew Street.
This will take you into St
Andrew Square. St Andrew is the
patron Saint of Scotland.

Towering over the square is **The
Melville Monument**. The column is

150 feet high and the figure on top is Henry Dundas (1742-1811), 1st Viscount Melville. He was a lawyer and the monument commemorates his work on electoral reform.

Cut across St Andrew Square and take the path leading right, away from the monument, to meet the end of George Street. Named after King George III, it was intended as the main thoroughfare and was planned to be wider than Princes Street (named after George's sons). It was conceived as a residential street but today it has many shops, bars, and offices connected with insurance and banking.

The seated man in the centre of the roadway is **James Clerk Maxwell** (1831-1879). He was a theoretical physicist and was best-known for his theories on electromagnetism.

Walk along the left-hand side of George Street. The very impressive Graeco-Roman style building was originally a banking hall designed by David Rhind, but is now **The Dome**, a rather smart bar and restaurant. It is worth popping inside to see the interior.

Opposite The Dome is **St Andrew's and St George's Church**, which is circular in design – so the devil has no corners in which to hide.

Pass The Hard Rock Café (or pop in if you like to collect their memorabilia) and in the centre of the next road junction is a statue of **King George IV**, who visited Edinburgh in 1822. Look closely at the statue and you will see he is wearing a 'very short' kilt. He insisted on wearing the kilt, but as his legs were not very good he also wore shocking pink tights to cover his knobbly knees.

Over Hanover Street, continue along George Street. On the left there is another impressive building with a pillared frontage, the **Assembly Rooms**. Built in 1783 to replace the Old Town venue, this is where every Thursday gentlemen 'reeled from the tavern flushed with wine, to an assembly of as elegant and beautiful women as any in Europe'. The ballroom is adorned with crystal chandeliers. During the interval of dances the guests were served oranges as refreshment.

The statue in the middle of the junction with Frederick Street is of British Prime Minister **William Pitt the Younger** (1759-1806). He introduced Income Tax and Window Tax. People were charged for the number of pieces of glass they had in their properties. This tax was known as 'daylight robbery!'

Nearing the end of George Street, at the junction with Castle Street, the statue here is of **Thomas Chalmers** (1780-1847) who led the disruption of the General Assembly of the Church of Scotland in 1843 and created the Free Church of Scotland.

Where George Street joins Charlotte Square, glance up left and right to the first floor levels of the buildings to see windows painted in black and white. They are known as **Pitt's Portraits** after the Window Tax – literal daylight robbery!

Turn right into Charlotte Square and the Oxford Bar is in Young Street, the first turning on the right.

Arthur's Seat and Holyrood Park

The 650 acres of Holyrood Park has some surprisingly rugged scenery with a sense of remoteness and its lochans, craggy ridges and small glens definitely instil the impression that a little piece of the Scottish Highlands has been brought almost to the centre of Edinburgh. This is an immensely enjoyable circuit around an extinct volcano that last erupted more than 350 million years ago, with the most stupendous views and through parkland that has a long history of royal patronage.

Start	Finish	Distance	Refreshments
Scottish Parliament, at the foot of the Royal Mile	Palace of Holyroodhouse	3 miles (5km)	Palace of Holyroodhouse Cafeteria

Arthur's Seat

ON THIS WALK

Scottish Parliament building	Queen's Drive	Dunsapie Loch
Holyrood Park	St Margaret's Loch	

Start by the **Scottish Parliament Building** at the foot of the Royal Mile. This modern-style building was opened on the 9th October 2004 by Queen Elizabeth II to house the Members of the Scottish Parliament (MSPs). The building caused a lot of controversy. Originally budgeted at £40 million, the cost rocketed to over £400 million. The choice of Spanish architect Enric Miralles, rather than a Scottish one, was also a bone of contention. The building schedule over-ran by three years, but despite these issues the Parliament is up and running and the building has received many awards and accolades including the Centenary Medal from Edinburgh Architectural Association, the Manuel de la Dehesa 'Premio De Arquitectura', and the Royal Institute of British Architects' Award. It is open to the public and you can have a guided tour, and enjoy the shop and cafeteria.

Walk along Horse Wynd, past the Parliament building, to find a white canopied structure on the right. This is **Our Dynamic Earth** exhibition. It is open to the public and tells the story of the creation of the planet through the various major geological periods from the Big Bang to the present day and beyond. It is a fascinating place to visit with lots of interactive displays (visited on Walk 11).

The expansive parkland ahead has its origins in volcanic fire dating to more than 350 million years ago.

Subsequently the area has been carved out and shaped by glacial ice. Human activity and occupation of the area began as the climate warmed to end the last Ice Age around 10,000 years ago. The park was part of the sanctuary of Holyrood Abbey and was first enclosed by King James V in 1540.

You may be curious about the name **Holyrood Park** and its origins. Way back in the 12th century there was a vast woodland here, Drumsheugh Forest, and it was popular with King David I of Scotland and his court for hunting. The story is that one day he was out hunting with his courtiers when he became separated from the group. A huge red deer stag came out of the woods and frightened the King's horse, throwing the King to the ground. The stag was going to attack the King when all of a sudden a miracle happened. A crucifix appeared on top of the stag's head between its antlers, and the stag then ran away. That night when the King was asleep he had a dream in which he was told to build an abbey to give thanks for his life being saved so miraculously, so he built the Abbey of Holyrood, the Abbey of the Holy Cross – 'rood' is a medieval word for a cross. You can visit the large abbey ruins beside the Palace of Holyroodhouse. The Palace is the Queen's official residence in Edinburgh.

As you walk into the park, the Palace on your left, turn left on to Queen's Drive, a wide

| Hunter's Bog | St Anthony's Well | |
| Arthur's Seat | St Anthony's Chapel | St Margaret's Well |

roadway with paved walkways on each side. This is a pleasant level walk. **Queen's Drive** was built on the orders of Prince Albert, husband and Consort to Queen Victoria, as part of his improvements to the park in the 1840s. This area had been a parade ground and in 1860, the Royal Scottish Volunteer Review was held before 100,000 spectators.

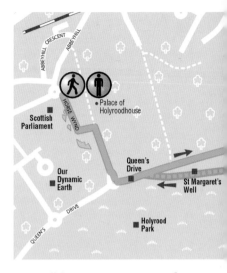

Farther along on your right you will come to **St Margaret's Loch** ('loch' is a Scottish word for 'lake'). This loch was also created by Prince Albert and is home to a variety of geese, swans and ducks, and there are pigeons too, feeding on the titbits brought by visitors. Take care as sometimes some of the birds can get a little over enthusiastic in their search for a tasty morsel.

At the end of the loch take the narrow road up to the right. There is a paved pathway on the left-hand side of the roadway which has one-way traffic, vehicles only travelling up the hill. Climbing this gentle incline you will begin to see some of the east side of the city.

There is also a lot of gorse here. You may have encountered it on one of the other walks. Dark green in colour, it is an evergreen shrub with sharp spines and a pretty yellow flower. There is a saying in Scotland 'when the gorse is in bloom it is the kissing time'. Luckily in Scotland it blooms all year long. If you get close enough to a cluster of the flowers you will find it smells like coconut, but be careful of the thorns.

St Margaret's Loch

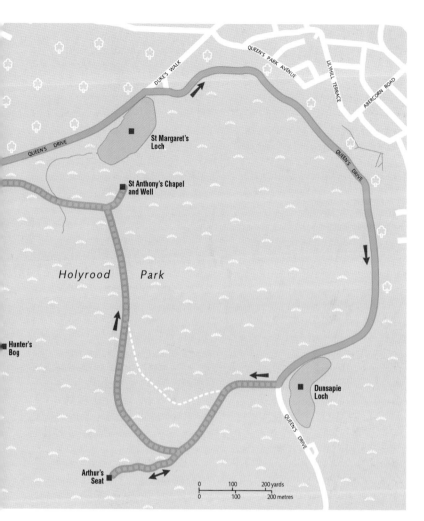

You are likely to meet other walkers, dog-walkers and joggers on this part of the route as many people enjoy taking exercise in Holyrood Park, fortunate that they have such a wonderful place to enjoy their leisure activities.

Follow the Queen's Drive pathway as it curves around the hill to another area of water, **Dunsapie Loch**, again home to a variety of birds including swans, which pair for life.

You are now nearing the summit of your climb, **Arthur's Seat**.

The name is nothing to do with King Arthur and Camelot, but is said to have originated from the Gaelic of Ard-na Saigheid – the 'height of the arrows' or 'hill of the archers', which would explain fortifications found here dating from around 2,000 years ago. These include remains of an Iron Age fort and tools and weapons have been found from this period close by.

Leave Queen's Drive at the bend and take the well-worn rough path to the summit. Take your time; the view from the top is well worth the scramble.

The summit is 251 metres (822 feet) above sea level and the panoramic views are quite stunning. More than a million people a year now visit the park and most of them make it to the top of Arthur's Seat. Drink in the scenery. On a clear day you can see right across the Forth of Forth to the north of the city and the coastline of the Kingdom of Fife. The magnificent view of the city is spread out before and you should be able to spot the Palace of Holyroodhouse, Our Dynamic Earth Exhibition Centre, The Scottish Parliament building and Edinburgh Castle on top of its own volcanic rock.

There is a tradition in Edinburgh that some hardy souls get up very early on the 1st May to climb to the top of Arthur's Seat to wash their faces in the morning dew. It is supposed to keep you young and your skin looking fantastic. The poem 'Auld Reekie', written by Robert Fergusson in 1773, contains the lines:

'On May-day, in a fairy ring,
We've seen them round St Anthon's spring,
Frae grass the caller dew draps wring
To weet their een,
And water clear as crystal spring
To synd them clean'

One man who truly believed in good health and extreme cold applied to Edinburgh's Town Council in 1783 to build a house on top of Arthur's Seat. Dr James Graham's planning application was refused.

In 1836 a group of five little boys out hunting for rabbits around the crags of Arthur's Seat found 17 miniature coffins containing small wooden figures. Their purpose has remained shrouded in mystery ever since, but some believed they were made for witchcraft. More recent speculation suggests that they may have been connected with the murders committed by Edinburgh body-snatchers Burke and Hare. The coffins are now displayed in the city's Museum of Scotland in Chambers Street.

After you have taken your fill of the views, the descent is via a different route. Retrace your steps a short way and then take the wide grass track to your left, heading down into the valley. As you go down the hill, on your left is an area known as **Hunter's Bog**. In 1564, Mary Queen of Scots created an artificial loch as an area for her courtiers to enjoy. Eventually, the Royal Hunting Forests were cleared and replaced by sheep. Some of these sheep were rather territorial, one blackface ram in particular. The Scottish blackface sheep has large, hard curled horns and knows how to use them if disturbed. In the autumn of 1740, some off-duty Redcoat soldiers were poaching some of the wildlife when they were unceremoniously butted from the rear by the sheep. The clerk of the court wrote 'it was observable of this malevolent beast that he always bore a malevolent eye to Redcoats; he'd often leave the flock on seeing a soldier and lend him a hearty bounce'!

You are quite safe today as there are no longer any sheep in the park. There is a Royal Park Rangers Visitor Service which was started in 1999, originally they were called Holyrood Park Constables, and charged with educational and environmental duties as well as law enforcement. One of their lesser-known responsibilities is to protect the catch-fly flower, a plant of the genus Silene or Campion, which also happens to be the official flower of Edinburgh. The rangers are sometimes called out to rescue climbers who find Arthur's Seat and Salisbury Crags a little more of a challenge than they initially anticipated.

Keep to this grassy path until you come to a track leading to the right. Make your way along it to the ruin you saw from a distance at the start of the walk. **St Anthony's Chapel**, built during the 13th century, was a place of pilgrimage for travellers. It also became a place of sanctuary, initially for criminals then latterly as a safe place for debtors. Unexpectedly, for a building in such a prominent location whose construction must have been witnessed by many people, surprisingly little is known about the origins of the chapel.

St Anthony's Chapel

From the 1100s ownership of the land was divided between the Abbeys of Kelso (in the Scottish Borders) and Holyrood. The chapel was linked to Holyrood by a well-made stone track with kerbstones that can still be seen in places. About three-quarters of the way along this ancient walkway there is a spring and a carved stone bowl known as **St Anthony's Well**. It has been suggested that the chapel may have been built as a landmark for pilgrims sailing up the Firth of Forth on their way to Holyrood. You can see the River Forth quite clearly from this historic vantage point.

The pope paid a grant for repairs to the chapel in 1426 but by 1560, after the Reformation, the chapel fell into disuse and disrepair. The remains that you see today are the north wall and part of a smaller building called a hermitage which may have just been used as a store room. The original building may have had a three-storey tower on the west side.

Make your way back to the pathway and walk down the hill by **St Margaret's Well** which is one of seven holy wells within the park. Cross the grass in front of St Margaret's Loch and return along Queen's Drive towards the Palace and Scottish Parliament Building.

For refreshments, the Palace of Holyroodhouse has a lovely cafeteria/restaurant with a good selection of hot and cold food. The cafeteria is in the outer courtyard of the Palace. An alternative is to walk up The Royal Mile for a few paces to Calarinda's on the right-hand side.

Stockbridge and the Royal Botanic Gardens

WALK 9

This is a gentle wander through Edinburgh's New Town village of Stockbridge with its specialist shops, cafés and quaint houses. The walk's centrepiece is the Royal Botanic Gardens, begun in the 17th century by two obsessive plant collectors and added to by successive Victorian plantsmen who travelled across the expanding British Empire in pursuit of their quests, the result of which are the marvellous gardens, landscapes and glasshouses in today's 70-acre site.

Start	Finish	Distance	Refreshments
Queen Street – Frederick Street junction	The Oxford Bar, Young Street	3¾ mile (6.3km)	Terrace Café (Botanical Garden); The Oxford Bar

Royal Botanical Gardens

ON THIS WALK

St Stephen's Church	The Colonies	Victorian Tropical Palm House
	Stockbridge	The Botanical Gardens

Start in Queen Street, at the junction of Queen Street Gardens West and Frederick Street, facing downhill towards a large church. Walk down the road, gardens on both sides, crossing Heriot Row and heading straight towards the church.

St Stephen's Church is the most significant landmark in the area. It was designed by William Playfair and was built between 1827 and 1828 for £18,975. Its great tower is 162 feet high and the clock contains the longest pendulum in Europe. The design was controversial and one professor said it looked like 'a mouth without cheeks', referring to the huge entrance with no lateral support on each side.

At the church, turn left into St Stephen Street, with St Vincent's Episcopal Church (built in 1857), on the left. Walk along St Stephen Street to reach the heart of the New Town village of **Stockbridge**. It is a settlement of ancient origin straddling the Water of Leith on an old livestock route into Edinburgh over the Stock Bridge. Mills and tanneries were clustered around the bridge and remnants of these still survive. Livestock were forded across the Water and for many years there used to be an old wooden toll bridge for pedestrians. Today's substantial stone bridge was built in the late 18th century.

Stockbridge has many quaint shops, bakeries, cafés, pubs and antique emporiums, and has become quite bohemian in appearance.

Sir Henry Raeburn (1756-1823), the portrait painter, made Stockbridge fashionable commissioning quality shops and exceptional country villas and terraces by the Water. He bought two estates and then developed large parts of the area and one of the residential streets is named after his wife - Ann Street.

At the end of St Stephen Street turn right on to Kerr Street then, at the junction, cross into Deanhaugh Street.

At the end of Deanhaugh Street the road splits, take the right-hand road into St Bernard's Row. This street was originally built in 1820 but the modern apartments with the balconies were built in 1982 on the site of an old cinema. This opened in 1911 as **The Palace** and was renamed St Bernard's Picture Palace in 1912. In 1921 the name was changed again to The Savoy and again in 1960 to The Tudor. By the 1960s there were financial difficulties and the cinema closed.

Later St Bernard's Row curves to the right, leading into Glenogle Road. On the left is an interesting residential area known as **The Colonies**. It consists of 11 tightly-packed parallel closes of terraced houses and

	Inverleith House		Fettes College	
Temperate Palm House		Inverleith Park		Ann Street

apartments. The Colonies was built from 1861 by the Edinburgh Co-operative Building Company and is the largest of the Victorian pioneering housing schemes. This building company was founded by a small group of masons in April 1861 and the company provided accommodation for 10,000 individuals, creating low-cost housing for working people, largely skilled artisans, over a period of 15 years.

Each house had a plot 20 feet square in the front and the use of a communal green. The advertisement for the area read 'a goodly town, surrounded by picturesque scenery and containing within itself every helpful and elevating influence'. Each family had a separate entrance: at ground floor level from the east, and up external stairs from the west to the two upper floors. The keystones of the ground floor windows are carved with tools of various trades.

On the right-hand side at the start of Glenogle Road there is a large red sandstone building. This is **Glenogle Baths** designed by Robert Morham in 1897. It is an old-fashioned Victorian swimming pool.

Now retrace your steps a little back to the junction with St Bernard's Row and turn sharp right into Arboretum Avenue. Follow this quaint street up to Inverleith Terrace then dog-leg left and right into Arboretum Place. Up on the right you will find the impressive western entrance to the Royal Botanic Garden in the form of the John Hope Gateway.

Botanist **Dr John Hope** (1725-86) was the inspiration for the 2009 western

gateway into the gardens. In 1761 he took on the joint appointments of Professor of Botany and Materia Medica at Edinburgh University and King's Botanist and Superintendent of the Royal Botanic Garden Edinburgh. He introduced the rhubarb plant to Scotland. Enjoy the gallery and exhibitions and maybe lunch in the splendid Gateway restaurant before exploring the gardens.

The Royal Botanic Garden is Scotland's national botanic garden, one of only two financed with grant-in-aid from the British Government – the other is Kew Gardens in London. It has its origins in the Physic Garden established near the Abbey of Holyrood in 1670 by two Edinburgh doctors, Robert Sibbald (1641-1722) and Andrew Balfour (1630-94). The two gentlemen met in France after travelling around Europe. They leased a plot of land at Holyrood, but their travels widened as the British Empire expanded and their collection of plants multiplied. The garden eventually moved to Inverleith in 1820 and it took three years to transplant the entire collection of mature trees, shrubs and plants. As the Garden grew it gained the grounds of Inverleith House for the arboretum and land belonging to the Caledonian Horticultural Society for the Rock Garden. The plant collection continued to increase through the expeditions of the Scottish plant hunters in the 19th and 20th centuries.

Now the Royal Botanic Garden covers 70 acres with a number of feature gardens. It is home to the largest collection of Chinese plants of wild origin outside China in the **Chinese Hillside Garden**. There is the **Scottish Heath Garden** which recreates the

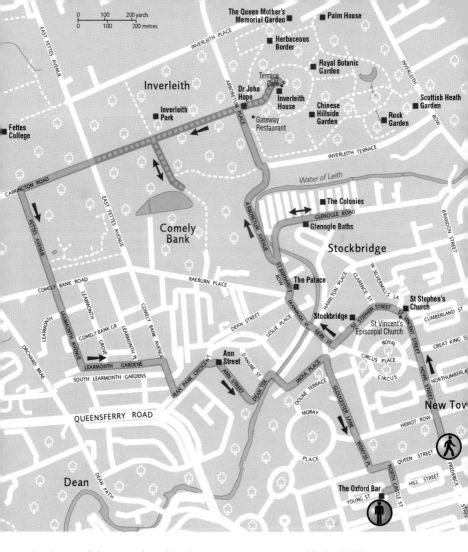

landscape of the Scottish Highlands. **The Rock Garden** has over 5,000 alpine plants. **The Herbaceous Border** has a century-old Beech hedge. **The Queen Mother's Memorial Garden** is a tribute to Queen Elizabeth the Queen Mother, the present Queen's mother, who had a great love of gardens and flowers.

There are also more than 25 glass-houses providing the correct climatic conditions for the collections of warm temperate and tropical plants. The first glasshouse, **The Victorian Tropical Palm House**, the highest in Britain, was built in 1834 at a cost of £1,500. An extension was added in 1862 at a cost of £6,000, to become the **Temperate Palm House**. By the 1960s these glasshouses were falling into disrepair and were replaced. The glasshouses were filled with topsoil that had been removed from the construction site of the Forth Road Bridge, which opened in 1964. The main glasshouse is on two levels with five climatic zones. There are ten glasshouses open to the public. The Plant and People House is home to the giant water lily, Victoria Amazonica, which opened its first flower in time for the official opening by HRH Princess Margaret in October 1967.

Inverleith House

Inverleith House, within the Gardens, built in 1774, was originally the home of the Scottish National Gallery of Modern Art (1960-1984) and now has changing seasonal art exhibitions for invited artists.

There is a lot to explore in the Royal Botanic Garden and you can spend many delightful hours here, even feeding the squirrels and pigeons, or visiting the gift shop. Refreshments are available at The Gateway Restaurant, which serves breakfast, lunch and afternoon tea, and at The Terrace Café.

Once you have explored the Gardens, make your way back to the John Hope Gateway. The gate will lead you out on to Arboretum Place. Cross the road into Inverleith Park.

Inverleith Park was purchased in 1899 from Mr Charles Rocheid for £33,500 and at that time also included a farm. The park plays an important part in the community and has three football,

four rugby and six seven-a-side pitches, a cricket square, petanque area and a children's play area. It is large enough to accommodate allotments for gardeners, a large pond with a landscaped 'marsh' area and a Sundial Garden. The park hosts around 400 events each year.

Keep ahead on the path through the park to a path junction. The route continues straight on to the Park's west gate, but do take this opportunity to explore or to feed the ducks. Exiting the west gate leads on to East Fettes Avenue.

Cross over into Carrington Road. Walk to the large, impressive gates on the right-hand side which lead into **Fettes College**. To perpetuate the memory of his only son William, who had predeceased him in 1815, Sir William Fettes (1750-1836), a former Lord Provost of Edinburgh and wealthy city merchant, bequeathed the then huge sum of £166,000 to be set aside for the education of poor children and orphans. As part of this bequest the school was founded in 1870. It is sometimes referred to as a 'public school', although this is the term traditionally used in Scotland for state schools, and Fettes is known as 'the Eton of Scotland'. An all-boy's school until 1970 when female pupils were first admitted to the final year classes, Fettes has been fully co-educational since 1983. The school has boarding pupils as well as day pupils. The main building by David Bryce blends the design of a French chateau with elements of the Scottish Baronial style.

The author Ian Fleming, creator of James Bond 007, wrote in *You Only Live Twice* that the agent attended Fettes College, his father's old school, after having been removed from Eton. There was a real life James Bond who did attend Fettes and he was a frogman with the Special Boat Service, much as the fictional character Bond has a naval background. The school had his *Who's Who* entry copied and framed over the Second Master's office door.

Another fictional character, Captain Britain, later to become Marvel Comics' Captain Britain, was actually Brian Braddock who attended Fettes College. Other notable Old Fettesians are Tony Blair, Prime Minister of the United Kingdom from 1997-2007; Tilda Swinton, screen actress and Oscar winner; and Michael Tippett, composer.

With your back to the gates of Fettes College walk up Fettes Avenue, opposite, until you reach the junction with Comely Bank Road. Head straight across up the hill on Learmonth Avenue. At the top turn left into Learmonth Gardens, then take a right into Comely Bank Avenue. Carry on up to Dean Park Crescent, turn left here, and then right into Ann Street, along which it really does feel like walking back in time to the 19th century. Stop for a moment and try to imagine the street with no cars and just the sound of horses' hooves and carriage wheels on the roadway, maybe the chatter of young ladies as they pass with the swish of their satin and damask gowns.

Ann Street is named after the wife of Henry Raeburn, the portrait painter. He actually gave the street to his wife as a birthday present. It is an exceptionally fine example of a 19th century Edinburgh residential street. The houses of different sizes are set back behind lovely gardens and make for a very picturesque street.

At the end of Ann Street bend left with the road into Dean Terrace, then turn right, crossing over the Water of Leith on to India Place. Follow this out to Gloucester Street and turn right. Walk up the hill along Gloucester Lane to Wemyss Place which leads back to Queen Street, just one block along from the start of your walk. If you now cross Queen Street and walk halfway up North Castle Street, then turn right into Young Street, you will find one of Edinburgh's most famous pubs. The **Oxford Bar** has been refreshing locals for many years, and is much favoured by writers, especially Ian Rankin, creator of Inspector Rebus. Do not be put off by the less than salubrious exterior, as they say on their own website, 'you can't judge a book by its cover'.

Leith

WALK 10

Even today some of the locals in Leith would prefer to call themselves 'Leithers' rather than residents of Edinburgh. This walk is to Edinburgh's port, until the 18th Century the main point of entry into Scotland, its significance declining after the union with England in 1707. Leith has been a frontier town, a trading post, a whaling haven and an armed city with its own parliament, and this is reflected in the surviving architecture of its churches, merchant's town houses and shops.

Start	Finish	Distance	Refreshments
St Mary's Cathedral, at the top of Leith Walk	Ocean Terminal or St Mary's Cathedral	4½ miles (7.6km)	Fisher's Restaurant; The Royal Deck Tea Room

Sculpture by Sir Eduardo Paolozzi, outside St Mary's Cathedral

ON THIS WALK

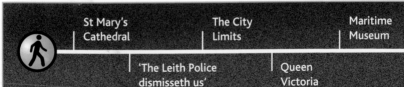

St Mary's Cathedral

The City Limits

Maritime Museum

'The Leith Police dismisseth us'

Queen Victoria

This exploration of Leith begins north of Waverley Station at the top of Leith Walk at the Picardy Place roundabout outside **St Mary's Cathedral.** This Roman Catholic cathedral dates from 1813 and was designed by James Gillespie Graham. The unusual sculptures outside the cathedral are by Sir Eduardo Paolozzi (1925-2005), born in Leith, and the eldest son of Italian immigrants.

Many of the surrounding buildings date from 1825 but on the right-hand side of the road is **The Playhouse Theatre** dating from 1927. Next to it is **The Glasshouse Hotel** contained behind the 1846 frontage of the original church which stood on the site.

From the Cathedral steps head for the left-hand side of Leith Walk, passing the Playhouse opposite, and soon after the next roundabout reaching **Gayfield Square**. This is now mostly private residences but is also home to the local police station. In Edinburgh there is a popular saying which might once have been used to determine if one had had too much to drink – 'The Leith Police dismisseth us'. Try saying it without slurring your words... maybe practise over the rest of the walk.

Keep going down Leith Walk. Cross over the junction with McDonald Road and at the next major junction with Pilrig Street you will see a beautiful church,

Pilrig Street St Paul's Church. It was built in 1861 and has very fine sandstone carving.

Opposite, on the right-hand side of Leith Walk, there is a pub called **The City Limits.** Its former name was The Boundary Bar and it marked the boundary between neighbouring Leith and Edinburgh. Many years ago each district had its own licensing laws; when drinking time was called at 10.00pm those enjoying a beverage on the Edinburgh side of the bar could cross over to the Leith side for an extra half hour's drinking. The drinking laws are very different nowadays.

Cross over Pilrig Street and keep ahead down Leith Walk. After you have passed Balfour Street there is another bar/pub called **The Volunteer Arms** which featured as a location in the film *Trainspotting*.

At the foot of Leith Walk there's a major road junction. **Queen Victoria** visited the area in 1842 and the statue here commemorates the event. The Queen kept diaries of her travels and in her *Journal of our Lives in the Highlands 1848-61* she wrote the following:

'Saturday 3rd September
The view of Edinburgh from the road before you enter Leith is quite enchanting; it is, as Albert said 'fairy-like', and what you would only imagine as a thing to dream of, or to see in a picture. There was that

| Water of Leith | | The Signal Tower | | Royal Yacht *Britannia* | | Crabbie's Warehouses | | Dr Andrew Bell | |

beautiful large town, all of stone (no mingled colours of brick to mar it), with the bold Castle on one side, and the Calton Hill on the other, with these sharp hills of Arthur's Seat and Salisbury Crags towering above all, and making the finest boldest background imaginable. Albert said he felt sure the Acropolis could not be finer; and I hear they sometimes call Edinburgh 'the modern Athens'. The Archers Guard met us again at Leith, which is not a pretty town.
The people were most enthusiastic, and the crowd very great. The Porters all mounted, with curious Scotch caps, and their horses decorated with flowers, had a very singular effect, but the fishwomen are most striking-looking people, and are generally young and pretty women – very clean and very Dutch-looking, with their white caps and bright coloured petticoats. They never marry out of their class.'

Negotiate this junction and make your way towards the large, modern shopping centre. Located behind the New Kirkgate Shopping Mall opposite South Leith Parish Church is **Trinity House**, which was built in 1816 originally as a hospital by the Fraternity of Masters & Mariners of Leith for the welfare of seamen. At the back of Trinity House are stones from another building that was on the site in 1555. Trinity House is now a **Maritime Museum** and is open to the public from Tuesday to Saturday and displays a great wealth of Leith's seafaring history and many fine paintings.

Return to the front of the New Kirkgate Mall by the Queen Victoria statue and turn down the street on your left. This is Constitution Street and was Leith's other main commercial thoroughfare. Walk on to the junction with Baltic Street and Bernard Street. On the right-hand side is **Leith Exchange**, which dates from 1809 and **The Assembly Rooms**, which were built in 1783 to house the dancing assemblies and social gatherings.

Turn left and walk along **Bernard Street**. There is some very fine architecture in this area. The former bank, built in 1804, has a large domed roof and **The Corn Exchange**, built in 1863, has a splendid front porch. You will also see a statue of Robert Burns, the famous Scots poet.

At the end of Bernard Street you reach what looks like a wide canal, but is in fact the Water of Leith. Here turn right and walk down The Shore. The first settlement at the mouth of the **Water of Leith** was probably prehistoric, but the earliest documented evidence shows that there was a settlement in this area in 1143. The port grew over the centuries and was Scotland's main port until the middle of the 19th century dealing in sugar, timber, grain, flax, paper, iron, whisky, wine and whaling. The profits from this trading went into the coffers of the city of Edinburgh from 1329 onwards when Leith became the official port of the burgh of Edinburgh.

Shipbuilding became the main employer in Leith in the 17th century and Scotland's first dry docks were built in 1720. In 1698 the Darien Expedition set sail from Leith. This consisted mostly of Edinburgh merchants trying to find an overseas outlet for Scottish

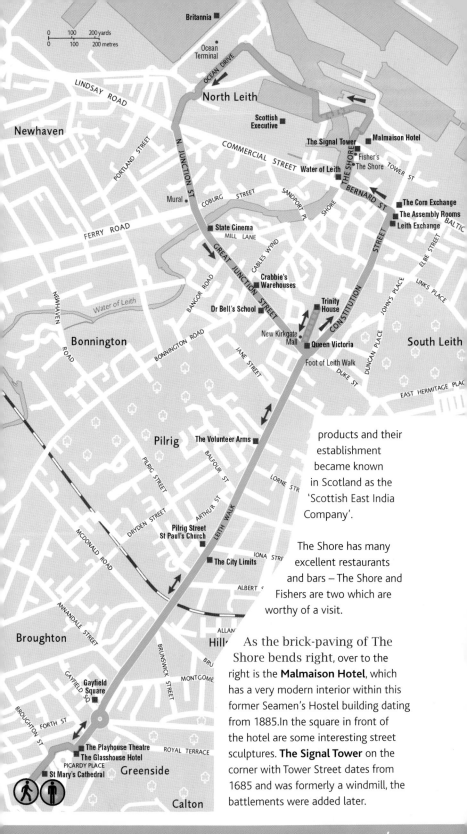

products and their establishment became known in Scotland as the 'Scottish East India Company'.

The Shore has many excellent restaurants and bars – The Shore and Fishers are two which are worthy of a visit.

As the brick-paving of The Shore bends right, over to the right is the **Malmaison Hotel**, which has a very modern interior within this former Seamen's Hostel building dating from 1885. In the square in front of the hotel are some interesting street sculptures. **The Signal Tower** on the corner with Tower Street dates from 1685 and was formerly a windmill, the battlements were added later.

Step across the square and through the gates on the other side into Tower Place. On reaching the roundabout turn left along Ocean Drive and then, to cross the Water of Leith, you must use the Victoria Swing Bridge. Once across, turn right and then left, back on to Ocean Drive. On your left, on Victoria Quay, is the modern **Scottish Executive** building, built in 1992. A lot of work is being done to regenerate this area with new apartment blocks and, as you will see shortly, a new shopping mall. Ahead of you is the Ocean Terminal, designed by Sir Terence Conran, a huge centre with over 70 shops, a cinema, restaurants and cafés and the Royal Yacht *Britannia*. You will not be able to see *Britannia* at this point as it is berthed behind Ocean Terminal, and you must enter the complex to access the ship.

Inside Ocean Terminal, *Britannia* is well signposted. You can use the elevator or escalator to reach the *Britannia* level. There you will find the ticket office and entrance into the exhibition prior to boarding the ship.

The **Royal Yacht *Britannia*** was built on the River Clyde at Glasgow, on the west coast of Scotland, in 1953. The yacht was decommissioned on 11th December 1997 and was given a home by the Forth Ports Authority in Leith, to be open to the public and for hire for corporate events. The exhibition displays the history of Royal Yachts with an insight into the lives of the crew, and the Queen and her family, on board. At the end of the exhibition audio handsets are available for self-guided tours around the ship.

A real treat on *Britannia* is to have morning tea or coffee, lunch or afternoon tea in the Royal Deck Tea Room. You have had a good walk and deserve to sit down for a while. Strongly recommended, it is a chance to relax and look out on to the harbour and River Forth from the beautiful glass sided restaurant. All the food is delicious and you can imagine being treated like royalty as you enjoy the facilities.

It was no ordinary life for a sailor on board *Britannia*. The crew were volunteers chosen from the general service of the Royal Navy. Their orders were nothing less than to 'strive daily for perfection'. Each sailor was hand-picked to meet the very highest standards and it was an honour and privilege to serve on board.

To preserve peace and tranquillity on board – orders were given by hand, soft soled plimsoll footwear

The Shore, Water of Leith

was worn to reduce noise and any work near the royal apartments had to be completed by 8.00am. The crew was to be as unobtrusive as possible; should by chance any crew member encounter one of the royal party, they were instructed to stand still and look straight ahead until the Royals had passed. There were 20 officers and 220 Royal Yachtsmen or 'Yotties' on board. The junior yachtsmen had the arduous task of scrubbing the two-inch thick teak decks each day to keep them in pristine condition. Many Yotties turned down their natural promotion to other Royal Navy ships to stay in their existing rank on board *Britannia*. Therefore promotion for the Yotties became known as 'Dead Man's Shoes' waiting for the post holder to retire. Once you have visited the rest of the ship make your way back to the shop in the visitor centre to hand in your audio handset.

If you feel you cannot walk back up into the city, albeit on a different route, there is a Britannia Shuttle Bus that takes you from the Ocean Terminal to Waverley Bridge, by Princes Street.

To continue the walk, leave the Ocean Terminal and turn right. Make your way up Ocean Drive to the traffic lights at the junction with the main road. Cross the road and walk up North Junction Street. Approaching the next major road junction, look behind you to see a large mural on the gable end of the right-hand terrace, which depicts scenes in the life of Leith. Continue straight on into Great Junction Street.

Soon on the left is the old **State Cinema** built in 1939, a very different architectural design to the rest of the surrounding area. It once contained a cinema, four shops and two billiard saloons, a skittle alleyway and – within the cinema – constantly moving coloured holophane lighting reflected off silver, green and ivory walls.

Beyond the junction with Bonnington Road, on your left, there are former bonded warehouses with small windows, many barred, which date from 1810. These were the **Crabbie's Warehouses**. Crabbies Green Ginger is still available today, a tasty drink on its own with ice or it can be added to whisky. These buildings were where whisky was kept secure for the Customs and Excise. Many of these have now been made into apartments or offices.

On the right is **Dr Bell's School** dating from 1839. Dr Andrew Bell (1753-1832) was an educationalist. He became Chaplain to the East India Company in Madras in 1787 and was given charge of the Madras Male Orphan Asylum; unable to find enough suitable teaching staff he devised a system of mutual tuition by the pupils which proved very popular and effective. He returned to Britain in 1797 and published details of his 'Madras System', which by the time of his death had been adopted by 10,000 British Schools. Madras College in St Andrews was founded in 1832 with a bequest of £50,000 by Bell himself.

Walk to the end of Great Junction Street where you'll re-join Leith Walk. Go right and retrace your steps to the top of Leith Walk.

Edinburgh's Museums

WALK

11

There are many fascinating and first-class museums in Edinburgh. This walk links six of them indulging you in many diverse subjects: geology and childhood, Scottish literary treasures and military history, and the past lives of Edinburgh's working class citizens. For museum lovers this walk could take a week; otherwise use different sections of the walk to pick out one or two museums at a time – an ideal walk for a wet day, presenting the opportunity to steal away indoors.

Start	Finish	Distance	Refreshments
Castle Esplanade	Our Dynamic Earth	1½ miles (2.6km)	Tower Restaurant (Nat. Mus. of Scotland); Clarinda's Tea Room

Field Marshal Haig, National War Museum of Scotland

ON THIS WALK

The National War Museum of Scotland	George IV Bridge	William Chambers
The Writers' Museum	The National Museum of Scotland	

Start on the Edinburgh Castle Esplanade. Go into the castle grounds to find **The National War Museum of Scotland**. *(Admission to the museum is included in the entry fee for the castle)*. This wonderful museum tells 400 years' of Scottish military history that has shaped the nation. There are uniforms, insignia, medals, diaries, photographs, paintings, videos and stories of heroism, victory and loss. One captivating story is of 'Bob', the brave little dog who was the regimental mascot of the 1st Battalion of the Scots Fusiliers from 1853-60. The dog served with them throughout the Crimean War and chased spent cannonballs. He has been preserved by the art of taxidermy along with a set of elephant toes belonging to the regimental pet of the 78th Highlanders. In 1838 the regiment returned from Ceylon (now Sri Lanka) with the elephant they had adopted. It lived in Edinburgh Castle and the keeper used to take it to the canteen where they both consumed their fill of beer and then retired to the stables to sleep off their hangovers together. The exhibits include exquisite embroidery work by soldiers passing time whilst on active service, and you can hear the skirl of bagpipes, used to encourage soldiers as they marched along.

Leave the castle and walk down the Esplanade and then Castlehill. Continue down the left-hand side of the Lawnmarket section of

Bob, the regimental mascot

the Royal Mile to the narrow entrance of Lady Stair's Close. Turn left along the passage to reach a courtyard and Lady Stair's House. This is the home of **The Writers' Museum**. This was the main museum of Edinburgh history from 1907 until Huntly House opened in 1932. The Writers' Museum displays items with a literary connection to the lives and work of Robert Burns (1759-1796), Sir Walter Scott (1771-1832) and Robert Louis Stevenson (1850-1894).

Robert Burns has been adopted by the Scottish people as 'their poet'. He was born on the 25th January 1759, and on each anniversary, in Scotland and throughout the world, Burns Suppers are held to celebrate the life and work of the ploughman who became one of the world's most well-known poets. He was a son of the soil, a farmer

| The Netherbow Port | | The People's Story Museum | |
| The Museum of Childhood | | The Museum of Edinburgh | Our Dynamic Earth |

who loved reading and never stopped educating himself. He had the ability to speak directly to the ordinary people in his verses. It was his own experiences that brought his poetry to life.

He was a great humanitarian and sympathised with the poor and oppressed. Burns deplored all manner of cruelty and the arrogance arising out of privilege and wealth. He was also fond of animals and wrote poems about a mouse, an old horse and a wounded hare.

Burns adored women. He had fifteen children, nine born out of wedlock, but he looked after all of them. The love of his life was Jean Armour whom he married at the age of twenty-six. They thought of emigrating to the West Indies but instead he went to Edinburgh where he was hugely acclaimed. He then toured Scotland as Caledonia's Bard, but he still needed to make money for a 'rainy day' so he became an exciseman and earned up to £70 a year.

He had recurring bouts of rheumatic fever and had strained his heart from farm labouring as a young man, which took its toll on his body, and he died at the age of thirty-seven in poverty. On the day of his funeral, his pregnant wife had no money, but he was given a grand military funeral with an instrumental band playing the 'Dead March in Saul'. Huge numbers of people gathered to pay their respects to this extraordinary genius.

When you come out of the museum retrace your steps to the Lawnmarket, in the Royal Mile. Turn left and at the crossroads turn right along **George IV Bridge**, named after the King in honour of his visit

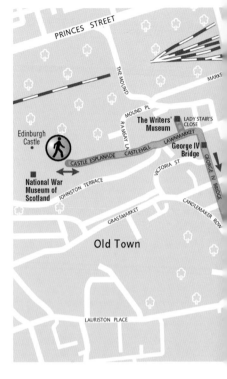

to Edinburgh in 1822, past the modern Missoni Hotel building. King George IV's visit was planned by Walter Scott. He was then knighted for his work. The bridge was built as a broad elevated street on 9 arches, but only two can be seen. The construction caused the loss of John Dowie's Tavern which sold Younger's Edinburgh Ale, a rather potent beer that almost caused the drinker's lips to become glued together.

Keep ahead along George IV Bridge, cross over Victoria Street and past the Central Lending Library, on your right, built in 1887. On the opposite side of the road is The National Library of Scotland built in 1934. Occasionally they have special exhibitions open to the public; if so there will be posters outside with details.

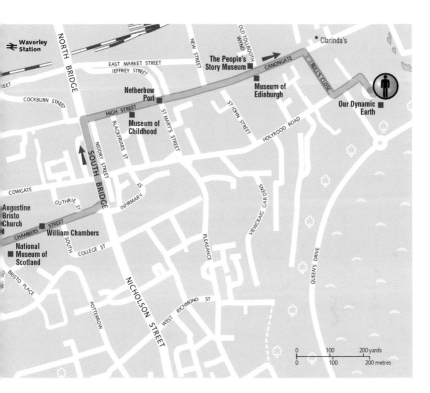

Cross to the left-hand side of George IV Bridge, soon walking past the **Augustine Bristo Church** built in 1837, with its wedding-cake style steeple. Reach the corner with Chambers Street. Chambers Street was named after the Lord Provost William Chambers, whose personal crusade had been to improve health conditions in the Old Town area of the city. There's a statue of the man himself in the middle of Chambers Street a little farther down on your left. Directly on the left is the Sheriff Court built in 1888. Across Chambers Street is the modern entrance to The National Museum of Scotland.

The National Museum of Scotland was built between 1861 and 1864 and the original building is impressive and elegant with grand entrance steps. The more recent extension has been faced

in sandstone so it will blend in with the older stonework. This is the largest museum in Britain outside London. It was founded as an Industrial Museum in 1854 and then renamed the Museum of

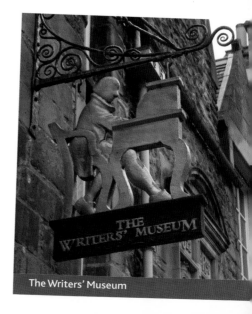

The Writers' Museum

Science and Art in 1864. The stunning main hall has cloistered galleries and an arched-rib timber and glass roof which allows the maximum use of daylight. In 1904 the building became The Royal Scottish Museum, until 1985 when the National Museums of Scotland united their offices. Later, this walk will take you to the other museum. The National Museum of Scotland has a huge variety of collections ranging from fossils, Egyptian, animal skeletons, ceramics, glass, Mary Queen of Scots' artefacts, engines, in fact too much to list but there is sure to be something to interest everyone and there is a café.

After leaving the museum, walk along Chambers Street past the statue. **William Chambers** (1800-1883) started work at the age of 13 as an apprentice to an Edinburgh publisher. In 1832 he printed and published the Edinburgh Journal, a weekly magazine, with his brother Robert as editor. They wrote the Chambers' Encyclopaedia between 1859 and 1868 in 520 weekly parts. As Lord Provost of the city he concentrated on slum clearance and promoted a scheme for renovating parts of the Old Town, including the long-awaited restoration of St Giles Church, for which he met the entire cost of £30,000. He died three days after the completion of the work and the first service in the church, after the official re-opening, was his own funeral.

At the end of Chambers Street, on your right, are some Edinburgh University buildings known as Old College built in 1789 by Robert Adam and completed by William Playfair. Turn left into South Bridge. This was constructed in 1786, a 19-arch viaduct, but now only one of the arches is visible. Continue along South Bridge to meet the Royal Mile. Here turn right and keep to the right-hand side of the High Street section of the Royal Mile.

On the corner is the Bank Hotel built in 1923. This was a bank between the two World Wars but was converted in 1992 into a Chicago-style speakeasy bar with hotel rooms above. Next to the Bank Hotel is Niddry Street. In 1591, this was where Provost Nicol Edward entertained James VI of Scotland and his wife Anne of Denmark.

On the opposite corner of Niddry Street is the Radisson Hotel, built in the 1990s in the style of the Old Town buildings, but inside it is an ultra-modern hotel. Just past the Radisson cross Blackfriars Street. This street was the site of Blackfriars Monastery which was bequeathed by Alexander II to the Dominican monks in 1230. The first printing press in Scotland was operated at the foot of this street by Chepman and Myllar in 1506. A little farther on the right is the Museum of Childhood.

The Museum of Childhood was created in 1986 and contains toys, books, games and other memorabilia associated with childhood. The original curator, Joseph Patrick Murray, founded the museum after he heard of two dolls, once owned by Queen Victoria, which were heading for London as there was no place in Scotland to display them properly. This is traditionally a playful place. Here in 1760, a child Jane, later the Duchess of Gordon, was seen riding on a sow pig which one of her sisters moved along with a stick. The museum is filled with wonderful exhibits of childhoods past. Although seeing a toy in a glass case that you may have played with when you were younger could make you feel a little old, you can relive childhood memories and admission is free.

Once you have completed the museum visit, turn right and continue down the Royal Mile. The next crossroads is the **Netherbow Port**. This was an old gateway into the city and its position is marked by brass plates imbedded at the crossroads.

Cross over and continue down the Royal Mile all the way to **The Museum of Edinburgh** opposite Canongate Kirk. Also known as the Huntly House Museum, it traces the history of Edinburgh from prehistoric times to the present day. The museum houses the archaeological finds from Cramond that describe the life of the Roman occupation in the east of Scotland 2,000 years ago. Another exhibition tells of everyday life in the Old and New Town areas of the city from the mid 18th century with extensive collections of pottery, glassware, silver and decorative art. There are many important items such as The National Covenant, the petition signed in 1638 demanding religious freedom and also the collar and dog bowl belonging to Greyfriars Bobby, the devoted little Skye terrier (see Walk 6).

Across the road is **The People's Story Museum** housed in the Canongate Tolbooth, which dates from 1591. This ancient building has been a tax office, jail and council office but now contains displays about Edinburgh's citizens at work and play from the 18th century to

Museum of Edinburgh

present day. Exhibits include a wartime kitchen, a bookbinder's workshop and the original Tolbooth jail.

Keep ahead down the Royal Mile, to reach Bull's Close on the right-hand side. Turn into this narrow alleyway and walk right through to Holyrood Road. Here go left and walk towards the unusual modern building with a sandstone base and huge white canopy.

Our Dynamic Earth looks like it has just parachuted into the city, but was built in 1999, on the site of a former William Younger Brewery. Inside is an interactive and virtual reality centre which takes you on a journey through our planet's past, present and future with impressive technology and 3- and 4-D experiences. You can travel back in time, through the Big Bang, the Ice Age, feel a glacier and the sticky heat of the rainforest, and come face to face with an extinct dinosaur- all in one building.

Bruntsfield

WALK 12

Escape from the city centre bustle on this walk to green parks and quiet residential streets on the south side of Edinburgh. Scotland is the home of golf and Bruntsfield was Edinburgh's first golf course. On this walk you can visit the original course's '19th green' and find out about some of the eccentric early players of the game. Discover, too, the literary and educational legacies of other notable Bruntsfield residents.

Start	Finish	Distance	Refreshments
Tollcross, the junction of Earl Grey St, Brougham St and Home St	Tollcross	1¾ miles (2.8km)	The Golf Tavern; Cobbs

The Golf Tavern

ON THIS WALK

Bennet's Bar	Bruntsfield Links	'Cock o' the Green'
Barclay Church	The Golf Tavern	

Begin the walk at the busy main road junction of Tollcross, where the A700 and A702 meet to the south-west of the city centre. Locate Home Street and walk along it towards the high steeple of the church in the distance.

On the left-hand side you will come to one of Edinburgh's best-loved theatres, **The King's Theatre**, built in 1906. Made of red sandstone in a Baroque style of architecture, the interior is classic Edwardian with wonderful galleries and glasswork.

Next door to the theatre is **Bennet's Bar**, one of the most famous 'watering holes' in the city. It has one of Scotland's finest bar interiors with Jacobean mirrors and tiled Arcadian pictures, all dating from 1891.

Follow Leven Street all the way up to the spire of Barclay Church, dating from 1864 and one of F T Pilkington's greatest achievements. Frederick Thomas Pilkington (1832-98) was one of the more interesting 19th century Scottish architects. He was a convinced Gothicist and was heavily influenced by the English High Victorian Movement. His church designs were eclectic, fusing medieval and 19th century influences to produce wonderful buildings. He was equally skilled at designing large country houses for the middle classes. The church was named after Mary Barclay who died in 1857 and she had willed a trust for the erection of a Free Church of Scotland building.

Turn left in front of the church along Glengyle Terrace and immediately right to walk with the church, right, and the park on your left. This lovely open grassed area is Bruntsfield Links, which remains a reminder of the ancient Burgh Muir and occupies a very special place in the history of Edinburgh for the pursuit of the Royal and Ancient game of 'gowf'. **Bruntsfield Links** was Edinburgh's earliest golf course. The famous Royal Burgess and Bruntsfield Links Golfing Societies originated here, both now have their own courses elsewhere.

There were a number of real characters associated with this course. Alexander McKellar was known as the **'Cock o' the Green'**. His golfing enthusiasm was an obsession. He was the owner of a tavern in the Georgian New Town, the managing of which he left to his long-suffering wife. Immediately after breakfast he would head off to Bruntsfield Links regardless of the weather. He would golf all day and in the darkness of the winter months was aided by the light from a lantern held by a very patient friend. He had taken to the sport later in life and was keen not to waste any time.

His wife would bring his meals to the links, but being engrossed in the game his food would often remain uneaten.

	James Gillespie's High School	St Margaret's Convent	
Willie Gunn	Dr Sophia Jex-Blake	Warrender Baths	

His wife, not surprisingly, developed a dislike for the game and any golfers who went to the McKellar Tavern when she was on duty were not made welcome. He played golf every day except Sunday, the Sabbath, as he was the door-keeper of an Episcopalian Chapel. One Sunday a gentleman in the church congregation placed a ball marker in the collection plate instead of a coin and this was quickly retrieved by McKellar. Despite the hours he spent on the golf course he never attained great prowess and was not a member of the Bruntsfield Golfing Society. He died in 1813 and proudly retained the title of 'Cock o' the Green'.

Now no golf course is complete without its '19th green' and Bruntsfield was no exception. Continue past the church and on your right you will come to the oldest known golf pub in the world, founded in 1456, **The Golf Tavern**. The tavern was previously known as the Golf Hotel. During its early history, purpose-built clubhouses did not exist and the local inns provided a place for meetings and social functions. Ye Olde Golf Tavern was used as Bruntsfield Links Society Club-house from 1788 until the early nineteenth century when they moved to Mussel-burgh, a little to the east of the city.

The Bruntsfield Links were also used by horse trading shows, travelling fairs and even grazing livestock. By the 19th century the Links had become so congested that the golf clubs decided to move outside the city to Musselburgh.

Alexander McKellar was the Links' most enthusiastic golfer but caddie **Willie Gunn** was the most eccentric. Willie Gunn arrived in Edinburgh from the

Highlands in 1780 and travelled around Edinburgh selling religious artefacts. He often stopped at Bruntsfield Links to watch the golfers. One day, caddies were in short supply and a player asked Willie Gunn to carry his clubs. He was rewarded with the payment of one shilling for one hour's work. Willie enjoyed this new found employment and took lodgings near the links. He paid his rent regularly and survived on a diet of bread and milk, never eating hot cooked food or having a fire in his room. He led a very frugal existence so he would be able to save enough money for his burial and funeral when the time came. He had a horror of having a pauper's grave.

His eccentric behaviour extended to his clothing. He wore all the clothes he possessed, both summer and winter. He wore several layers of undergarments, trousers and jackets, with the sleeves cut off, over which he had a red top coat, the official uniform of the Bruntsfield caddies.

When not employed caddying he would visit the village fairs and earn extra money by performing conjuring tricks. In the autumn, Willie would return to his home in the Highlands selling his religious artefacts on the way north. He would spend around six weeks out of the city then return to his caddying on the Links. In the autumn of 1820 he set out for the Highlands telling his friend Douglas McEwan, a golf club maker, that he now had enough money to ensure a respectable funeral. Willie never returned from the Highlands and no one was able to discover what had happened to him.

The kings (and one queen) of Scotland were among the distinguished participants of golf in earlier centuries, earning golf its reputation as a royal as well as an ancient game. James IV, Mary Queen of Scots, James VII, Charles I and Charles II all played. It is believed that while Charles I was playing at Leith Links, news came to him of the Irish Rebellion.

The accounts of the High Treasurer of Scotland for 1503 show a constant purchase of new golf balls... which makes one think that James IV was maybe not such a great golfer. In the reign of James VI (James I of England), making golf clubs had become an important craft and in 1603 he appointed William Mayne as a maker of bows, arrows, spears and golf clubs to the King. Golf ball makers were given sole rights to manufacture these and only balls with their special mark were to be used. The balls were made of leather and stuffed with feathers and in 1600 the cost was a fixed price of 'four schillings of this realm'.

Just past the tavern, where the road turns right as Barclay Terrace, cut the corner by taking the tarmac path to Whitehouse Loan, and continue left. Walk on past Warrender Park Terrace and then Warrender Park Road. The Warrender family has been associated with this area since 1695 when they acquired the Bruntsfield Estate.

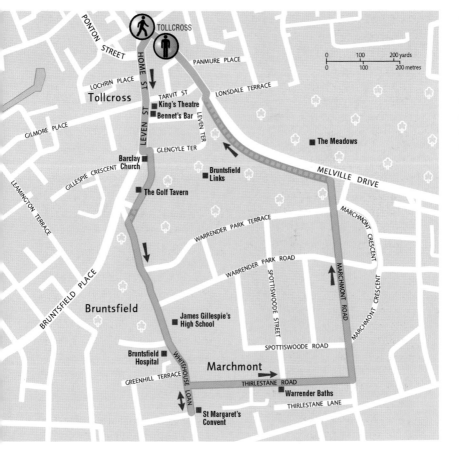

Farther along on the left are the walled grounds of **James Gillespie's High School**. James Gillespie (1726-1797) was born in Edinburgh. He opened a tobacconist shop in the High Street in 1759. He and his brother, John, bought a snuff mill with land attached and, in time, added more land to their portfolio. His motto was:

'*Wha wad hae thoct it
That noses had bocht it*'

This refers to snuff being sniffed from the hand into the nose, and he became a very wealthy snuff merchant. It had been his intention to bequeath a great deal of his wealth to 'a youth whom he had conditionally promised to make a man'. He stated in his will that his estate plus £12,000 should be devoted to the foundation of a hospital for the care of elderly men and women and an additional sum of £2,700 was left to establish a school 'within the City of Edinburgh or suburbs thereof for the education of 100 poor boys, to be taught reading, writing and arithmetic'.

Eventually James Gillespie's became a fee paying school for girls only, but in 1972 it became a comprehensive co-educational school. The novelist, poet and short story writer Muriel Spark (1918-2006) was born in Edinburgh and educated at James Gillespie's High School for Girls. She used the school as the model for the Marcia Blaine School in her book *The Prime of Miss Jean Brodie*. A British film of the same name was made in 1969 with Maggie Smith in the title role of teacher Miss Jean Brodie. Miss Brodie referred to her girl pupils as the 'crème de la crème'.

Continue along Whitehouse Loan and pass the older arched entrance into James Gillespie's. Opposite is a red sandstone building, now offices, that used to be the **Bruntsfield Hospital**, founded in 1858 by Dr Sophia Jex-Blake. She was one of the great pioneers among women doctors. The hospital was primarily a hospital for women and children.

Sophia was born in Hastings, Sussex, and educated at Queen's College for Women in London. She campaigned for women's higher education and studied medicine in New York from 1865-67. Barred, as a woman, from continuing her medical studies in England, she approached the Faculty of Medicine at Edinburgh University in 1869, and together with five other women, persuaded the authorities – against mass opposition from male students – to be allowed to attend lectures. Thus Edinburgh became the first British university to enrol women. Separate classes had to be held for male and female students which meant that professors had to duplicate their lectures, and with little extra payment many declined to oblige.

She pursued most of her medical studies in Edinburgh but was forced to

St Margaret's Convent

go to Berne to graduate as a Doctor of Medicine. She then gained the Licentiateship of King's and Queen's Colleges in Ireland, enabling her to practice in Great Britain. She was convinced that there were many women who would prefer to be examined and treated by a female doctor. She opened a ward of five beds at her dispensary; later the patients were transferred to Bruntsfield Lodge, Dr Jex-Blake's family home, which was on the site of the present building.

Soon after crossing Thirlestane Road, look for the magnificent arched entrance with a stone-carved knotted rope, on the left. **St. Margaret's Convent** was originally the mansion-house called the Whitehouse, which gave its name to the road you have been walking along, Whitehouse Loan. The original house was built in 1505, and it was in this year that the name Quhytehouse was first recorded. The Whitehouse was to become the first Roman Catholic convent to be established in Scotland after the Reformation. It was occupied by the nuns of the French teaching order, the Ursulines of Jesus, who afterwards opened it as a boarding school for girls. The property had a varied history until the early 19th century when it was purchased by Mr John Menzies of Aberdeenshire, a great benefactor of the Catholic Church in Scotland, for the establishment of a convent. Dedicated to St Margaret of Scotland, it was ready for occupation on December 26th 1834 and educated 'upper class' girls in the convent school.

The convent school is now The Gillis Centre (Archdiocese of St Andrew and Edinburgh) and houses the theological library of the former Gillis College.

Return to the junction with Thirlestane Road and go right; the wall of the convent on your right. Where the wall ends you come to the **Warrender Baths**. The name Warrender has been carried across the world by the members of Warrender Swimming Club. Records state that in 1843 a public meeting was held 'to further the opening of suitable baths for the working classes, the promotion of cleanly habits among the trades and working classes being essential for the removal of disease and the general improvement of that large and important class of people'. The baths were officially opened in 1887 and the Warrender Club was founded. David Wilkie swam here and went on to win the 200 metres breaststroke in the 1976 Olympic Games in Montreal. He was made a life member of the Club in recognition of his achievement.

At the end of Thirlestane Road turn left into Marchmont Road (refreshments at Cobbs at junction with Spottiswoode Road) and walk all the way down to the open parkland. Upon reaching Melville Drive walk left with the Bruntsfield Links on your left and the Meadows on your right. **The Meadows** is on the site of an extensive loch, which was drained in 1657 to provide an attractive public park. Many sports were enjoyed on the Meadows and the Royal Company of Archers used it for archery practise. Today it is still used for recreational activities and entertainment including the Meadows Festival each summer.

Follow Melville Drive back to Tollcross to complete the walk.

Duddingston Village and Loch

WALK

13

Originally a rural settlement, Duddingston still retains its village atmosphere despite being consumed within Edinburgh's eastern suburbs. It has an ancient church, a secret garden and a pub that lays claim to being Edinburgh's oldest. 17th-century village life was harsh for the rural poor and, as is revealed on this walk, misdemeanours were summarily punished, but at least today's visitors are spared the sheep's heads 'boiled or baked' on the pub's bar menu.

Start	Finish	Distance	Refreshments
The Royal Commonwealth Pool, Dalkeith Road	Royal Commonwealth Pool, Dalkeith Road	2¾ miles (4.7km)	The Sheep Heid Inn

The Sheep Heid Inn

ON THIS WALK

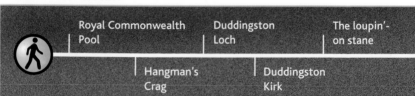

Royal Commonwealth Pool	Duddingston Loch	The loupin'-on stane
Hangman's Crag	Duddingston Kirk	

The walk begins at the **Royal Commonwealth Pool** located to the south of the city centre in the Newington area, at the junction of Dalkeith Road (A7) and Holyrood Park Road. Built in 1967, this is an Olympic-standard swimming and diving pool with seating for 1,000 spectators, used for the 1970 Commonwealth Games that were held in Edinburgh.

Walk along the side of the pool building on Holyrood Park Road. Shortly pass **Pollock Halls** on the right. These buildings are the halls of residence for Edinburgh University, built in 1959 around the much older Salisbury Green House, now a hotel, which dates from 1867.

Keep ahead towards the entrance to Holyrood Park. Just before the park gate on the left-hand side of the road, look out for the bright red **Victorian Post Box**. As you enter the park keep to the right-hand pavement and at the roundabout keep right on to the Duddingston Low Road. As you walk along here, way up to your left is the area known as **Samson's Ribs**.

Farther along Duddingston Low Road, down to the right is a golf course and a large white mansion. This is **Prestonfield House** which was built in 1687. It is erected on the site of a villa that was burnt down in 1681 during an anti-Catholic riot. Now a luxury hotel,

it is where rhubarb was first grown in Scotland and, as a tribute, inside there is a restaurant called Rhubarb.

Later on as the road bends, up on the left is **Hangman's Crag** or Hangman's Rock. This is the place where, back in the reign of King Charles II, one of the notorious executioners decided to end his own life, so troubled was he at putting to death many innocent and religious men. He was so overcome by the folly of his ways he fled from the city hoping to find peace and solitude in the park, but the next day he was found dead at the foot of the rock.

The old name for the area you are going to explore is Dodynstane, named by a Norman knight, Dodin, who rented the lands from the Abbott of Kelso, who had been gifted it by King David I in the 12th century.

Duddingston Loch is on your right. The first residents of the area lived in crannogs on the loch. A crannog is a wooden hut built on stilts in the water. The loch is the only example of a natural freshwater loch in the city of Edinburgh. It is now a bird sanctuary – Bawsinch and Duddingston Nature Reserve. The northern or village side is open all year long. Its waters and reed beds are an important site for breeding and over wintering wildfowl. Sit here for a while and watch the huge variety of birds. Imagine what it must have been like in centuries past during the winter

	Dr Neil's Garden		The Sheep Heid Inn		
The Jougs		The Causeway		Dr James Tytler	

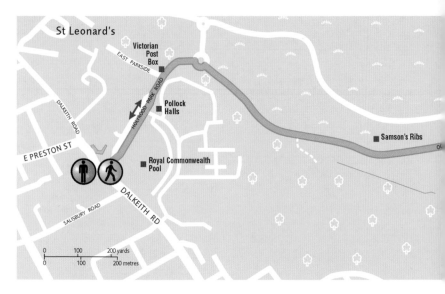

with skaters and curlers enjoying their sports on the frozen loch.

There is a very famous painting, *The Rev. Robert Walker Skating on Duddingston Loch*, by Sir Henry Raeburn, considered to be one of Scotland's best-known works of art. It portrays the Church of Scotland minister skating on this loch. The Reverend Walker was born on 30th April 1755 and as a child his father had been minister of the Scottish church in Rotterdam, so the young Robert almost certainly learnt to skate on the frozen canals in Holland. He was a minister of the Canongate Church in the Royal Mile as well as being a member of the Edinburgh Skating Club, the first figure skating club in the world. The club met on Duddingston Loch when conditions were suitable. You can view the painting in the National Gallery in the city centre (see Walk 15). There is a recent suggestion that the painting is actually by French artist, Henri-Pierre Danloux, rather than Raeburn, but this will be debated for a long time.

Beyond the park gate you come to Duddingston village. Up the hill on your right is **Duddingston Kirk**. The church dates from the 12th century and was originally built on a wooden promontory overlooking the loch. This is one of the oldest churches still in use today in Scotland. It was built by the monks of Kelso on the land gifted by King David I to the Abbot of Kelso. It is essentially Norman in design but there have been additions in the 17th century.

The jougs

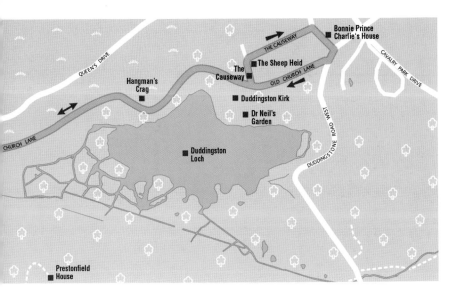

To the right of the church's entrance gate is the **loupin'-on stane**. This block is a short flight of rough stone (stane) steps leading on to a platform, set at about the height of the stomach of a horse. When the parishioners arrived at church on horseback they could dismount easily by using the stone block; it also made mounting, after the service, a lot easier. 'Loupin' is a Scots word for leaping or jumping.

Also notice the chain with a metal collar – **the jougs**. This iron collar and chain was used to mete out punishment for wrongdoers for a variety of offences: drunkenness, adultery, blasphemy and failing to attend the church services on Sunday. The victim would often be chained for a while then released and made to stand at the entrance to the church in sackcloth to ask God's forgiveness. While in the jougs they could also have rotten fruit and vegetables thrown at them.

Records of the time show that two people who were guilty of adultery were severely reprimanded: 14th October 1660, '...Susan Douglas adulteress with David Howeyson,

adulterer, being cited before the Session, confessed upon their knees and besought the Lord to pardon them of that great sin. The Session ordained them to begin their public repentance at the next Lord's Day and to stand at the Church door in sackcloth from the second bell to the last, after being released from the Joug Collar and thence enter the Church in sackcloth.'

The loupin'-on stane

The Manse (originally the minister's house), next to the church, now has the most wonderful secret garden known as **Dr Neil's Garden**. The garden is the result of dedication, imagination and a lot of hard work by Drs Andrew and Nancy Neil. They have turned what was a derelict piece of land in the 1960s into a haven of colour, beautiful terraces and rockeries incorporating azaleas, rhododendrons, magnolias, conifers, heathers and alpines. It is open to the public free of charge but donations are very welcome.

In one corner of the garden is the Curling Tower, designed by Playfair and built in 1825 for the Duddingston Curling Society to store its curling stones. The building is also known as Thomson's Tower because the upper room was used as a painting studio by the landscape artist the Reverend John Thomas, who was also the minister of Duddingston Church from 1805 until his death in 1840. So take your time to wander around and sit awhile in this lovely garden. The tower was his private haven and when unannounced visitors came to call at the manse, and he was working in his tower-based studio, his servant would inform the callers that his master was in Edinburgh.

To explore more of the village walk down **The Causeway**, the old village street, opposite the church. In the early part of the 18th century the village had around 500 residents. Many of the men earned a basic living carrying coal from the pits nearby to fireplaces throughout the city. Some of the women worked on looms, weaving coarse flax known as Duddingston Hardings for which they were paid 4 pennies a yard (a little smaller than a metre). The women who were unskilled at weaving were employed washing linen and carrying milk. The farmland around the village was quite fertile and in 1746 a ploughman could earn £3 a year. Living conditions were near squalor in damp and ruinous cottages.

The decline in the coal trade led to a fall in the population by 1800, but as the agricultural buildings were improved many villagers moved back to the land. Wages had doubled and the village began to develop with a school for 40 pupils, a library, post office and a Friendly Society. This Society, an early form of welfare support, could be joined for 5 shillings and quarterly contributions were paid; this ensured that members who were unable to work could receive sufficient funds to live.

As you round the bend, on the right-hand side sits one of the most famous pubs in Edinburgh, if not Scotland – **The Sheep Heid Inn**, translated as 'The Sheep Head'. Reputed to be Edinburgh's oldest surviving public house it dates from 1360. It is said that 'many opulent citizens resorted in the summer months to solace themselves on one of the ancient homely dishes of Scotland... sheep heads boiled or baked'. King James VI frequented the Sheep Heid in 1580 and presented an embellished ram's head and horns, which for many years adorned the bar area. The original silver-mounted ram's head had a small recess to hold snuff.

Although sheep's heads, boiled or baked, are not – as far as the author is aware – on the menu, other interesting traditions still survive. The old skittle alley is still popular and The Trotter's Club (founded in 1888 and originally composed of Edinburgh journalists) still

Bonnie Prince Charlie's house

meets regularly in the pub. The Sheep Heid has been feeding and watering visitors for more than six centuries so why not go in and enjoy being part of ancient Edinburgh history.

Once you venture out of the pub turn to the right and continue along the village street to round the next bend. On the left, look for quite a large house with five windows in the upper floor and a door with two windows on either side at ground floor level. There is a small plaque above the door. This was **Bonnie Prince Charlie's house** shortly before the Battle of Prestonpans in 1745. He held a council of war in the building.

Another famous resident of the village was **Dr James Tytler** (1745-1804). He was an author, encyclopaedist, chemist and balloonist. He had been a surgeon on a whaling boat but then moved to Duddingston village, often living in considerable poverty. Robert Burns described him 'in leaky shoes, a sky-lighted hat and unlikely breeches'. He was responsible for almost three-quarters of the Encyclopaedia Britannica. He built a printing press and turned out many copies of the Encyclopaedia at his home in Duddingston, as well as many other successful publications, but he was a poor businessman and never seemed to benefit financially from his work. In 1774 he was living on the Holyrood Abbey Sanctuary lands to escape his creditors.

Even his ballooning escapades in 1784 were not very successful. He eventually managed to rise to a height of 105 feet (32 metres) and descend again, which qualified him as Britain's first balloonist, but he was overshadowed by other more successful and more popular balloonists. His wife left him in 1775 when he was co-habiting with at least two women. These circumstances eventually led to a flight from justice for the crime of bigamy in 1788. He left his women friends and moved to the town of Berwick on the east coast.

Walk on to re-join Church Lane, turning right past the large mansions which are almost hidden behind the high garden walls. Once back at the church, follow the lane and rewind your way back through the park.

Morningside, Braid and Blackford

While some of its architecture has earned Edinburgh the accolade 'the Athens of the North', it shares with another Mediterranean capital, Rome, the rare geographic phenomenon of a city built on seven hills. Starting to the south of the city centre in the popular residential suburb of Morningside, this walk leads through the beautiful nature reserve of the Hermitage of Braid and climbs to the Royal Observatory atop Blackford Hill with more far-reaching views over the Scottish capital.

Start	Finish	Distance	Refreshments
Holy Corner, junction of Morningside Road and Chamberlain Road	The Braid Hills Hotel, Braid Road	5¼ miles (8.5km)	The Braid Hills Hotel, Braid Road, or The Canny Man's, Morningside Road

Agassiz Rock

ON THIS WALK

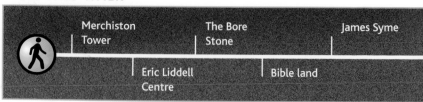

Merchiston Tower

Eric Liddell Centre

The Bore Stone

Bible land

James Syme

Begin the walk at Holy Corner, appropriately named as there is a church at each corner of this main road junction. Facing south, with your back to Edinburgh city centre, on your right is the Christ Church Episcopal Church (1878) and a little farther up the hill, the Baptist Church (1872) and on your left, the United Church (1927) and just across the road junction is the Eric Liddell Centre which used to be North Morningside Church (1879).

Start with a short diversion along Colinton Road. Walk up to Napier University on the right. Through the front of this building and into the courtyard there is a much older property, **Merchiston Tower**, which dates from 1495. This was the home of John Napier (1550-1617). He studied at St Andrews University from the age of 13 and became the 8th Laird of Merchiston five years later. He had a strong interest in mathematics and devised a system of logarithms as well as the world's first mechanical computing device, a series of numbered rods called Napier's Bones.

Return to Holy Corner and cross the road towards the Eric Liddell Centre on the corner of Chamberlain Road. North Morningside Church has been renamed the **Eric Liddell Centre** in memory of the sprinter and missionary (1902-45), known to the world through the film *Chariots of Fire*, who was a member of Morningside Congregational Church.

Now walk past the Eric Liddell Centre along the left-hand side of Morningside Road. The top of the hill marks the summit of the ancient Burgh Muir. On your left is a magnificent red sandstone building, the Church Hill Theatre, opened as a theatre on 25th September 1965 but originally the premises of the Morningside Free Church.

Keep ahead and walk downhill along Morningside Road as far as Newbattle Terrace. Just a few steps before the corner you will come to Morningside Parish Church, but look very carefully along the church wall on your left-hand side to find **The Bore Stone**.

The section of road along which you have just walked was for a long time known as Banner Place. This is a reference to the Royal Standard that was pitched in the bore stone to muster the Scottish Army on the Burgh Muir, prior to the Battle of Flodden in 1513. The stone had lain in a nearby field but was then built into the wall by Sir John Stuart Forbes of Pitsligo in 1852. This quotation is from *Marmion* by Sir Walter Scott.

'Highest and midmost was descried
The royal banner, floating wide;
The Staff, a pine tree strong and straight:
Pitched deeply in a massive stone
Which still in memory is shown,
Yet bent beneath the Standard's weight.'

The Hermitage of Braid

Blackford Hill

The Canny Man's

Hermitage House

Agassiz Rock

Down Newbattle Terrace, you can pick out the **Dominion Cinema** opened in 1938 and built in a flamboyant, Art Deco style by Captain WM Cameron.

Continue down Morningside Road. Glancing over to the right-hand side, notice the small building with a large clock, **The Old Schoolhouse**. This dates from 1823 and served the village population until 1892.

Farther down on the right-hand side of the road is **The Merlin**, built on the site of the old village blacksmith, Denholm Smiddy, which ceased working in 1900. This area was described in 1832 as 'a row of thatched cottages, a line of trees and a blacksmith's forge'. There is also the Morningside Library which was opened on the 9th November 1904.

Carry on down through Morningside. Beyond Falcon Road, a few of the streets have biblical names like **Canaan Lane**, **Jordan Lane** and **Nile Grove**. It has been suggested that Morningside's biblical names can be traced back to 1650 when Oliver Cromwell and his army occupied lands close by. It is thought that Cromwell's Puritan troops made many forays into this area, believing their altercations with the local people were similar to those of Joshua and the Canaanites. There was a house called Little Egypt which stood by the Jordan Burn (a burn being a small river). The village of Egypt is still found mentioned in documents from 1717. There is a small village around 20 miles from Edinburgh called Carlops where annual fairs were held and in some old papers found there, dated 1793, it states that a man called Israel attended the fair, 'Israel a man who lived at Canaan, Morningside, near

the lands of Egypt and the River Jordan in 1792, and whose children were known as the 'children of Israel...'; all very biblical.

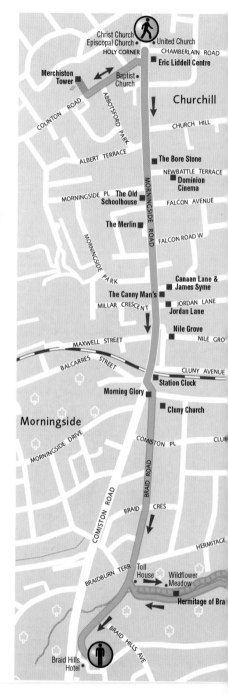

Reach the junction with Canaan Lane. In this street is a house called 'Millbank' which became the home, in 1842, of **James Syme** (1799-1870). He was a surgeon, but also dabbled in chemistry. He discovered a process for waterproofing cloth using a by-product distilled from coal tar that had properties for dissolving India-rubber, which could then be used to soak fabric to make it fully waterproof. Unfortunately he did not patent this discovery, but five years later Charles MacIntosh did, lending his name to the standard term for an overcoat made from waterproof fabric.

Between Canaan Lane and Jordan Lane sits **The Canny Man's** or Volunteer Arms, one of Edinburgh's most famous pubs. This was the original village inn. First known as The Volunteer's Rest or The Rifleman, it later changed its name to the Volunteer Arms or the Canny Man's

(canny meaning careful). At the end of the 18th century it was a two-storey building owned by James Kerr who built up a substantial group of regular visitors consisting of local people, farm labourers and the men of the Edinburgh Volunteers who practised their shooting in a field nearby at Blackford. You should really take some time and go inside as the interior is very, very different. It is akin to entering an antique shop that serves refreshments.

After visiting the Canny Man's continue along the main road, passing a small garden area after which Morningside Road opens out into a broad junction. This used to be Morningside Station which was opened to passenger traffic in 1884. The railway station is long gone, but you can still see the **station clock**, which was presented to the people of Morningside.

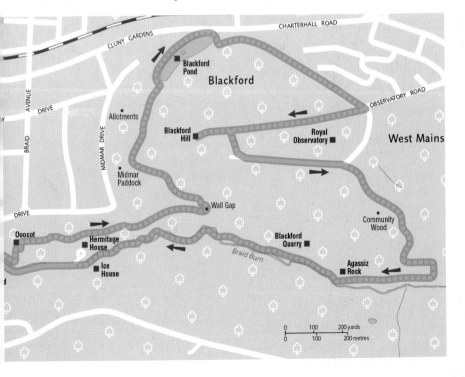

The Canny Man's

and the Braid Burn on your right to the Doocot (dovecot, a 'doo' is a Scottish word for a pigeon or dove). From the doocot follow the red route to the Visitor Centre in Hermitage House.

Alternatively, walk along the flat tarmac path from the Toll House until you come to the Visitor Centre and there pick one of the short paths through the wood to the red route and turn left to reach the doocot.

Straight ahead is the **Morning Glory**, formerly the Hermitage Bar, a place in which to sit and watch the world go by. To the left of this is **Cluny Church** where the first service was held on the 4th May 1890. The building cost £20,000.

Make your way up Braid Road between Cluny Church and Morning Glory. Continue for about 650 yards (600m) until reaching a mini roundabout at the junction with Hermitage Drive. Keep ahead on Braid Road and shortly come to the old Toll House, immediately after which there is a path off to the left into **The Hermitage of Braid**, believed to be named after a hermit's cell which was located here in the 17th century. It is now a wonderful nature reserve.

Here you have a choice of routes. If you have suitable footwear for the rougher, muddier pathways, follow the red waymarked route, through a gate on the left soon after entering the Hermitage of Braid. This leads past a delightful wildflower meadow on the left

The **Doocot** is the second largest example in Edinburgh and once contained 2,000 sandstone nesting boxes. It would provide a year-round supply of meat for the local landowner. The doocots were also a source of eggs and pigeon droppings. The latter was mixed with potassium nitrate to make a form of gunpowder.

Back in the 12th century, Henri de Brad lived in a tower house on the rocks above where Hermitage House now stands. The tower became a fortified castle, but all that remains is the doocot and parts of a walled garden. Raiders would often destroy a fortification but never the doocot as it would provide eggs and meat.

Hermitage House was built in 1785 for Charles Gordon of Cluny. In 1802 Alexander Campbell wrote that the building '...has an antique air well suited to the charms of the surrounding scenery and the fascinating beauties of this sequestered retreat'.

If you have followed the tarmac drive from the Toll House, as you approach Hermitage House there is a path off to the right that leads up to the 18th century **Ice House**, where ice was stored for use in summer, having been collected over the winter months.

After seeing the doocot and the Visitor Centre, continue on the red route through the woodland heading eastwards, with Hermitage House off to the right. Eventually come to a grassy field, Midmar Paddock, on your left. Continue along the winding path through the wood to reach a gap in a wall. Through this gap turn left to walk down the other side of the paddock until you come to the allotment gardens on your left-hand side. This now follows the nature reserve's blue route.

This route is taking you around **Blackford Hill** which is another of Edinburgh's volcanic lava remnants. Continue on the path to **Blackford Pond**, taking the path to the left of the pond. There are information boards about the birdlife that can be seen at the pond; the island in the middle is a nesting site, so it is a good place to stop for a while and relax.

You can break off from this walk by leaving the park by the exit close to the pond. This will take you out into Cluny Gardens. Turn left there and the road will eventually take you back to Morningside Road, by the Cluny Church and Morning Glory bar.

Otherwise continue past the pond and follow the blue route past the nature reserve car park. You will get superb views of the city of Edinburgh from this route. Follow the path right up to the radio mast and carry on to the impressive building with the copper domes on top of the hill. This is the **Royal Observatory** built in 1892. The observatory was originally on Calton Hill (see Walk 5), but was moved when light pollution there became a problem. The building is home to the UK Astronomy Technology Centre and the University of Edinburgh Institute of Astronomy. The observatory is not open to the public unless for a special event.

Leaving the observatory, stay with the blue route and walk past the golf course, follow it through the Community Wood, and then take the steps down into the glen. Keeping to the blue route turn right to walk past **Agassiz Rock**, named after Swiss geologist Louis Agassiz who in 1840 stated that the grooves in this overhanging cliff were the 'work of ice', the first recognition of glacial activity in Scotland.

Head past **Blackford Quarry**, which used to provide road stone from 1826-1953 and is now disused, to arrive at Scout Bridge, re-joining the red route. Follow it straight ahead, eventually passing the Ice House off to your left and regaining the tarmac drive to the Toll House. On leaving the Hermitage you can seek refreshments at the Braid Hills Hotel, up to the left. The hotel has a splendid spot right on the top of this hill, or you can turn to the right and make your way back down to Morningside. The choice is yours.

Edinburgh's Galleries

WALK 15

Edinburgh has a vibrant art scene. This route threads together a variety of venues where all manner of traditional and modern artwork is on display. Many of the galleries are housed in buildings originally designed for very different purposes including a church, a school and a fruit and vegetable market, which are of considerable interest in their own right. As with Walk 11 (Museums) this is another one you can dip in and out of on a rainy day.

Start	Finish	Distance	Refreshments
The Queen's Gallery, adjacent to the Palace of Holyroodhouse	Queensferry Street, at the west end of the city	4½ miles (7.5km)	Henderson's, 94 Hanover Street; Café Modern One (Modern Art Gallery)

Hinge detail, The Queen's Gallery

ON THIS WALK

| The Queen's Gallery | Fergus Art | The Royal Scottish Academy |
| The City Arts Centre | The Fruitmarket Gallery | |

Begin at **The Queen's Gallery** which is right next to the Palace of Holyroodhouse at the bottom end of the Royal Mile. The original building dates from the 1840s and was the former Holyrood Free Church and Duchess of Gordon's School, but it fell into disuse in the late 19th century. Architects were appointed in 1999 to create a visual theme to celebrate the Golden Jubilee of Queen Elizabeth II. The huge oak entrance doors have gilded bronze hinges decorated with the unicorn and scenes of Arthur's Seat, Salisbury Crags and the Royal Mile. There are also depictions of boughs of native Scottish trees like chestnut, oak, rowan and hawthorn. The stone archway is decorated with carved and gilded Scottish flowers including thistles and daisies. The gallery is purpose-built with a programme of changing exhibitions featuring many works from the Royal Collection. The gallery was officially opened by Her Majesty the Queen on 29th November 2002, as part of the Golden Jubilee celebrations.

From the Queen's Gallery walk up the Royal Mile for almost ½ mile (800m) to the junction with St Mary's Street and Jeffrey Street, here turning right. Follow Jeffrey Street as it curves round to meet Market Street and go left. Pass under the road bridge and soon come to **The City Arts Centre** on the left.

The City Arts Centre is housed in this huge Baroque Style warehouse which was built in 1899 and has one of the best collections of Scottish art. There is an escalator and elevator to help move you around the six floors. The centre has a nationally recognised collection of Scottish art and also new work from local and international artists. There are a variety of exhibitions throughout the year from early photography to contemporary art. There is also an excellent café and gift shop.

Fergus is a contemporary Scottish artist. His sculptures are created from debris, both industrial and beach-combed, the aftermath of fires and terrible tides, shattered by human nature's wasteful ways or the raw power of nature. His work is a gentle rebirth and by using Spanish colours he seeks to bring warmth and hope. As the hours of daylight shorten in late autumn, the output of his work multiplies in defiance of nature and by applying Mediterranean colours, the spirits are lifted in the artist and in those viewing his work. He is a devout disciple of Joan Miro and fellow countryman Picasso, who continue to inspire him greatly. He senses that the older he becomes the more colourful the work he creates.

'Above the slate-grey cloud, there is an azure sky.
That is where you'll find me'
Fergus 2012 www.fergusart.co.uk

	Henderson's		The Scottish National Gallery of Modern Art	
The National Gallery of Scotland		Dundas Street		Stewart's Melville College

Fergus Art

Just across the road in Market Street, you will find **The Fruitmarket Gallery**. Originally built as a fruit and vegetable market in 1938, it was transformed into an art gallery in 1974. The gallery exhibits contemporary, thought provoking and challenging art by both Scottish and international artists.

To resume the walk, continue along Market Street and turn right into Waverley Bridge. This bridge is over Waverley Railway Station, built in 1844. At the top of Waverley Bridge you will see a huge monument on your left, located in East Princes Street Gardens, the **Sir Walter Scott Monument**, built between 1836 and 1846, and designed by George Meikle Kemp. The monument is dedicated to the writer Sir Walter Scott who wrote 'Rob Roy' and ' Ivanhoe' amongst many other great works. In the base of the monument you will see a marble statue of Sir Walter with his deerhound, Maida, one of his 13 beloved dogs. The statues around the outside of the monument are characters from some of his writings. If you are feeling energetic you can climb the series of spiral staircases inside and make your way right to the top of the monument. There are viewing platforms to take in the wonderful vistas over the city. If you make it, there is a reward of a certificate to commemorate your climb of 287 steps to the top of this great Gothic rocket.

Stroll through the gardens to the next pair of galleries, **The Royal Scottish Academy** and **The National Gallery of Scotland**, located next to each other across the gardens. Edinburgh has the title of 'The Athens of the North' and you can see by looking at these two

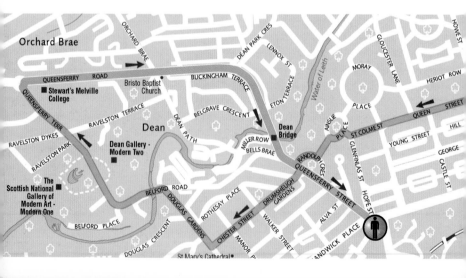

magnificent buildings that the title is well deserved.

As you approach the two buildings, the Scottish National Gallery is the left-hand one. It was designed by William Playfair in 1854. It is the second most-visited attraction after Edinburgh Castle. The gallery is made up of three interconnected buildings and is home to a major part of Scotland's sensational national collection of fine art. It houses European paintings and sculpture. In front of the National Gallery is the RSA, The Royal Scottish Academy, again designed by Playfair, in 1826. The Academy is one of Europe's finest venues for international exhibitions and the Garden's Entrance, which lies beneath the two buildings, connects them. It is like a huge temple with a statue of a very young Queen Victoria on top at the front, with sphinxes over the portico. The RSA houses some Old Masters and collections of the holders of RSA scholarships. There is also an excellent cafeteria and shop.

Exit the RSA building into Princes Street and cross this busy thoroughfare into Hanover Street. On the corner of this street you will see a gold-painted mail box. The post boxes are usually painted red, but this one was repainted gold to commemorate the achievements of Edinburgh-born **Sir Chris Hoy**, who is Britain's most successful Olympic track cyclist. He represented Great Britain at the London 2012 Olympics winning his sixth gold medal.

Walk up Hanover Street and go over the junction with George Street, and continue down the hill. It is worth making a slight diversion to investigate No. 94 Hanover Street. Here you will find **Henderson's**, much loved by artists, actors, writers and musicians. It has been hailed as a ground-breaking business that changed the nation – 'Eat Better, Live Better' – being their motto. The shop first opened in 1962 providing an outlet for the produce of Janet and Mac Henderson's East Lothian farm. The legendary basement restaurant soon followed and quickly became an Edinburgh institution. Today there is

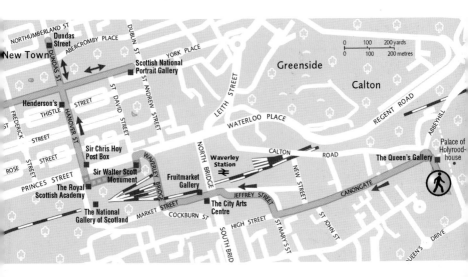

also a bakery, delicatessen and gallery. The laid-back atmosphere set against the backdrop of the **Janet and Mac Gallery** is a real cultural hub. Fergus Art is often on display; you may be lucky enough to see one of his exhibitions during your visit.

Returning to the walk, at the end of Hanover Street turn right on to Queen Street, here walking to the next junction North St David Street. The impressive building with statues and lamps on your right is the Royal College of Physicians built in 1845. Head towards the huge red sandstone building that is the **Scottish National Portrait Gallery**, built in 1863. Take time to look at the outside with numerous statues, which are all characters from Scottish history. Can you spot William Wallace and King Robert the Bruce guarding the entrance? This building has undergone a major internal refurbishment and houses portraits and landscapes and many other artefacts. The cafeteria is said to be one of the best in the city and there is also a shop.

When you come out of the gallery, if you wish to explore some of the city's smaller private galleries, turn left back to the junction with Hanover Street, but this time turn right down Queen Street Gardens East and on into **Dundas Street**. Here you will find some wonderful smaller galleries and shops such as The Di Rollo Gallery, The Phoenix Gallery, The Edinburgh Gallery, Bourne Fine Art and The Scottish Gallery.

Once you have quenched your artistic thirst in Dundas Street

make your way back up to Queen Street and turn right, walking to the west end of the street. At the very end it becomes St Colme Street. Keep ahead here, shortly bearing left into the oval of Ainslie Place. Turn left again into Great Stuart Street and follow this into Randolph Crescent, taking the right-hand curve. Once in Queensferry Street, use the pedestrian crossing then turn left and immediately right into Lynedoch Place, which very shortly continues as Drumsheugh Gardens and a little later as Chester Street. At the T-junction with Palmerston Place go right, but first look left to see the huge St Mary's Cathedral, built 1873-79, an episcopal church, and alongside it, St Mary's Music School built in 1885.

Walk down the hill and turn left over the Belford Bridge keeping on Belford Road to reach **The Scottish National Gallery of Modern Art**, erected in 1825.

This was originally John Watson's School, being converted in 1984. The collection is now divided between two buildings; the main building is now known as **Modern One** and just across the road is the **Dean Gallery**, built in 1833 as the Dean Orphanage, and now called **Modern Two**. Modern One features French and Russian art from the beginning of the twentieth century, cubist paintings and expressionist and modern British art. Special highlights include paintings by Matisse and Picasso. Modern Two houses a changing programme of world-class exhibitions drawn from the permanent collection. There is a recreation of Eduard Paolozzi's studio as well as his 7.3 metre tall sculpture – *Vulcan* – that dominates the café. Modern Two is also home to the gallery's library and archive, which is open to the public by appointment. There is the permanent work 'The Stairwell Project', a large-scale work by Turner Prize winner Richard Wright, comprising several thousand individually hand painted forms.

To re-join the route back up to the centre of the city, continue down Belford Road and on into Queensferry Terrace towards the roundabout. Here turn right along Queensferry Road. Just a short distance along you will see a magnificent building on your right, **Stewart's Melville College**, built in 1848. The school was opened in 1855 by the Merchant Company of Edinburgh, to whom Daniel Stewart, upon his death in 1814, left money and instructions that a hospital for the needy children of the city should be built. It was transformed into Daniel Stewart's College in 1870. Melville College was founded in 1832 by the Rev. Robert Cunningham and was originally named 'The Edinburgh Institution for Languages and Mathematics', but the name changed when the school was in Melville Street in the city's West End. The two schools merged in 1972 and now teach 700 boys and girls.

Continue past the college to reach the next crossroads, overlooked by Bristo Baptist Church. Here cross the main road to keep along Queensferry Road's left-hand side. You will get a tremendous view down

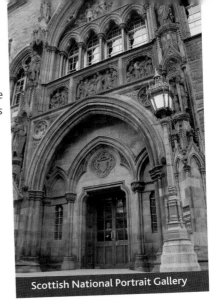

Scottish National Portrait Gallery

South Learmonth Avenue to what looks like a fairy castle, but is in fact Fettes College. Queensferry Road sweeps round a wide bend with Victorian terraced houses on both sides dating from the 1860s and 1870s in Learmonth Terrace on the left and Buckingham Terrace on the right.

Then cross **Dean Bridge**, which was built by the great engineer Thomas Telford in 1831. This bridge spans a 32m-deep (35 yds) chasm down to the Water of Leith. Cross the road at the bridge to look down into Dean Village which used to be a self-contained community with a meal mill and tanneries. Few of the original buildings survive and there are now many modern apartments. At the far end of Dean Bridge, on the right-hand side of the road, is a quaint little building called Kirk Brae House, which is a lodge and antique shop. The house dates from the 17th century but was baronialised in 1892.

Across Dean Bridge, head straight on into Queensferry Street to return to the West End of the city.

This book would not have been possible without the love for and from my mum and dad, Sybil and Jim McMurdo, who gave me a real appreciation of Edinburgh and Scotland, and my partner Ian Barquist, for his love and support while I wrote this book. I thank them all from the bottom of my heart; it has been a wonderful experience.

I would like to thank Mr Iain Hobbs who was a wonderful and inspirational mentor when I was studying to be a Scottish Tourist Guide. He brought the characters and colourful history of the Royal Mile alive on our many tutored walks around the Old Town.

Also, to thank my history teacher at James Gillespie's High School for Girls, Miss MacIntyre, whose history lessons were so full of fun and kept the whole class enthralled.

Walks: Devised and written by Margot McMurdo
Photography: Christopher Burns, Image Ecosse; and page 28 iStockphoto
Maps: Cosmographics Ltd
Design: Ark Creative (UK) Ltd

© Crown copyright / Ordnance Survey Limited, 2017
Published by Crimson Publishing Ltd under licence from Ordnance Survey Limited. Pathfinder, Ordnance Survey, OS and the OS logos are registered trademarks of Ordnance Survey Limited and are used under licence from Ordnance Survey Limited. Text © Crimson Publishing Limited, 2017

The right of Margot McMurdo to be identified as the author of this work has been asserted by her in accordance with the Copyright, Designs and Patents Act, 1988.

ISBN: 978-0-31909-034-3

This product includes mapping data licensed from Ordnance Survey
© Crown copyright and database rights (2017) OS 150002047.

While every care has been taken to check the accuracy and reliability of the information in this guide, the author and publisher cannot accept responsibility for errors or omissions or for changes in details given. When walking in Edinburgh it is advisable at all times to act with due care and attention, and anyone using this guide is responsible for their own well-being and safety.

This edition first published in Great Britain 2013 by Crimson Publishing and reprinted with amendments in 2017.

Crimson Publishing, 19-21C Charles Street, Bath, BA1 1HX

www.pathfinderwalks.co.uk

Printed in India by Replika Press Pvt. Ltd. 2/17

A catalogue record for this book is available from the British Library.

Front cover: Edinburgh Castle from Princes Street Gardens, ©iStockphoto

Title page: Ann Street, Stockbridge